LETTERS FROM
ST PETERSBURG

Victoria Hammond holds a Master of Arts in art history from the University of Melbourne and has worked as an art historian and curator of several nationally touring exhibitions. She is the award-winning author of several art catalogues and sponsored histories, and lives in Melbourne.

LETTERS FROM ST PETERSBURG

VICTORIA HAMMOND

ALLEN&UNWIN

First published in 2004

This project was assisted by the Federal Government through the Literature Fund of the Australia Council, the Victorian State Government through Arts Victoria, and a Varuna Fellowship granted by the Eleanor Dark Foundation.

Allen & Unwin
83 Alexander Street
Crows Nest NSW 2065
Australia
Phone: (61 2) 8425 0100
Fax: (61 2) 9906 2218
Email: info@allenandunwin.com
Web: www.allenandunwin.com

National Library of Australia
Cataloguing-in-Publication entry:

Hammond, Victoria.
Letters from St Petersburg.

ISBN 1 74114 338 1.

1. Hammond, Victoria — Journeys — Russia — Saint Petersburg. 2. Saint Petersburg (Russia) — Description and travel. I. Title.

914.721

Internal design by Zoe Sadokierski
Set in 11/16 pt Sabon by Asset Typesetting Pty Ltd
Printed by Griffin Press, South Australia

10 9 8 7 6 5 4 3 2 1

For Yvonne, Olga, Sasha and Liudmila

CONTENTS

And down the legendary embankment
Came not the calendar—
But the real Twentieth Century.

Anna Akhmatova

HELL AND ITS PROSPECTS

———◆———

I know no one. I don't speak the language. The city has a reputation for being dangerous. I've become addicted to this scenario, to the thrill of travelling alone and watching how, this time, I deal with the terrors of a strange place.

After years of arriving at foreign ports, airports, railway terminals, I've established a pattern that pushes fear into the background. I'm now a muddled old hand at deploying travellers' aids: guidebooks, basic conversation booklets, hotel listings at terminals. I arrive, I check the tourist information office, gather city maps, jot down hotel phone numbers and the Arabic or Italian for phrases like 'Do you have a single room available?' 'How much?' and 'What bus do I get to Piazza del Corso?' Then I ring two or three hotels, find the bus stop, panic about getting off at the right stop, get off at the wrong one, wander around in a labyrinth of streets, dragging my suitcase and furtively consulting the map (I'm hopeless at reading maps), and within an hour or so I'm usually experiencing delight or dismay at the hotel room I find my-self in.

But this time it's different. This time it's Moscow and my instincts tell me that in this gloomy, low-ceilinged cavern of an air terminal there is no tourist information office, no hotel register, no one who understands even basic English. It's six a.m. and, apart from a straggle of fellow passengers and a few officials, Scheremetsaya Airport is deserted. This time I haven't bothered with a guidebook or basic conversation book — Russian Cyrillic script is beyond me. In any case, they're unnecessary: Ada, a curator at the Russian Museum in St Petersburg, is meeting me.

At least I hope to god she's meeting me. As I shuffle along in the queue to have my passport stamped I become edgy. It's not just the dirty yellow light and sullen faces of the guards; there's a dull metallic echoing as if the invisible machinery of totalitarianism is still relentlessly operational; its rhythm gets inside my head and oppresses my thoughts. For the first time it occurs to me that my correspondence with Ada has been minimal: my introductory letter, hers welcoming my visit, mine with information enabling her to obtain for me an official invitation to Russia, and a final one from her saying she would fly from Siberia, where she planned to visit her ailing mother in Tomsk, to meet me in Moscow and accompany me to St Petersburg. By the time I faxed my flight details to the Russian Museum, it is likely she'd already left for Tomsk.

I shamble along, my head buzzing with fragmentary contingency plans. I take a perverse pleasure in this; sometimes, I lie in bed at night devising escape narratives, ways out of traps and labyrinths. The plan now is to get a taxi, ask to be taken to some hotel in the centre where someone speaks English, get the train to St Petersburg ... But how will I convey this to a taxi driver who speaks no English? I don't even know the Russian word for hotel. Besides, I've been warned about Moscow taxis, the Russian mafia, and other dangers of the kind that accumulate around exotic destinations to scare the pants off travellers.

By the time I'm watching bags and suitcases revolve on the carousel, I've resolved to trust to the process of putting one foot in front of the other — always on the alert, mind you — until a sequence of encounters and events leads inevitably to somewhere.

I've memorised Ada's face in Carlotta's photographs of her: long ash-blonde hair, delicate features, green eyes, aloof gaze. I head for the barrier gate, knowing the face won't be there. I'm impatient for these moments of anxiety to be done with so I can get on with the business of surviving Moscow.

She's standing right at the gate, anxiously scanning the crowd for my face. How beautiful she is, her blonde hair now in a short bob with a fringe. She's thin, vulnerable, not at all aloof like the photographs of her — not at this moment. We're both exclaiming with relief, laughing at having found each other so easily.

Outside the terminal, the early light is dull and the entrance, partly blocked off, has an impermanent feel. A solitary black taxi waits at the kerb.

'No. Don't get the taxi here.'

Is she, too, fearful of Moscow?

We pile into a battered minibus with a few tired-looking Muscovites, half of them wearing eighties-style black leather jackets with big pleated shoulders, and drive through nondescript outskirts for twenty minutes or so. Street corners with low-rise cement housing have a village feel and tufts of grass break through the bitumen. The bus suddenly stops in the middle of a rubble-strewn open space, drab tenement blocks in the far distance. The driver gets out, followed by all of the other passengers. This is the end of the line.

Ada alights and talks with the driver. I can see she has no idea where we are but doesn't want to worry me. I am nervous anyway, but in spite of her refinement there's something steel-like about Ada and I trust her to get us through this. We drag my luggage out of the bus and line it up on the weed-strewn rubble and stand there, bereft.

'What happens now?' I ask.

Ada makes a 'don't worry' gesture with her hands and glances left and right.

A boy rides past on a bicycle. Ada asks him something and he stops to answer, then rides off.

A couple of minutes later a rusty ute pulls up and Ada talks with the driver. It sounds like she's bargaining; her face takes on the set look with the disdainful little pout that I will come to know so well.

She smiles and nods at me to get in. The driver opens the passenger door, gets out and puts my luggage in the tray, returns to the driver's seat and we take off for Leningradski Station. I glance at Ada, mystified, and she explains that this is how Russians get around — the few who have cars give lifts to the majority who don't. She adds, with mild outrage, that this man wanted to charge us because he thought I was a tourist. She silences me when I protest that this is okay. It's a long drive to the station, so when we get out I slip the driver a 5000 ruble note (about 80 cents). He's overjoyed. She's silently furious. I come to learn that Ada takes pleasure and pride in negotiating on my behalf; she hates the thought of my being ripped off like a tourist, like an American.

While Ada buys our tickets to St Petersburg, I stand at the entrance of Moscow's monumental station, intrigued by the diversity of Russians. The crowd is similar to any capital city's, except the extremes of humanity are more exaggerated here: a pair of glamorous girls in cripplingly high-heeled boots stride up the steps past pitiful beggars, sightless or limbless casualties of Afghanistan or earlier wars. High above the heads of pedestrians a gigantic Max Mara banner flaps in the breeze. Capitalism comes to Russia.

On the train north to St Petersburg, sitting in a compartment with four others, Ada and I talk into the night. We discuss our mutual friend Carlotta, an artist who has visited Russia three times and arranged this visit to St Petersburg for me. Carlotta is a romantic whose art feeds off adventure and isolated places. Hence her love affair with Russia.

'Carlotta tells the most wonderful stories about Russia,' I say to Ada. Wonderful in their fusion of terror and comic absurdity, like the time she flew from Siberia to St Petersburg — then Leningrad — in 1990, just before perestroika. The cost of the airfare for a non-Russian was prohibitive, so, on the basis that they bore a physical resemblance to each other — fair hair and skin, heavy-lidded blue eyes — a Russian artist offered Carlotta the use of her passport. The artist had a squarish face, so they wrapped a thick scarf around Carlotta's face and neck to hide her heart-shaped one. Because Carlotta knew very little Russian then, she improvised a kind of sign language to convey to officials that she was a deaf-mute. At the planning stages this was Carlotta's favourite kind of adventure, thrilling and amusing — Mata Hari meets the Marx Brothers — as well as eminently practical — she was saving a lot of money she didn't have — but when the time came to show the passport, she was terrified. At one point an official stared so sternly at her face and the passport and back to her face, her knees went to water. By the time she boarded the plane, so old and rusty, she was shaking with fear, so she began to pretend she was a bit twitchy and simple as well. They sat her at the back of the plane.

A man boarded with his dog, a big Siberian mountain dog. They sat it next to Carlotta. She loves animals and at first she didn't mind, but it kept slobbering all over her and it was one of those dogs that are always pawing you for attention. Of course she was unable to give it a voice command, so she spent the entire trip whacking it on the nose. Six hours. At lunchtime she was given a meal. As soon as she removed the plastic, the dog gulped down the lot.

She arrived in Leningrad hungry and terrified, swearing never to use the Russian artist's passport again. But she did. She used it on the boat to Valaam and two or three other times. And each time she was petrified.

I'm smiling as I tell Ada which story I'm thinking about.

'Such stupid, dangerous thing to do,' says Ada, shaking her head and looking out at the flat twilit landscape flashing by. 'I say to her I prefer to know nothing of such arrangements.'

I wonder if Ada has a sense of humour. Surely she must if she's a friend of Carlotta's. 'I have this clear image of Carlotta,' I prompt, 'flying high above the clouds in a rusty, rattling plane, her face half-hidden in a big scarf like a peasant, fighting off the attentions of an amorous dog.'

The ghost of a smile hovers around Ada's mouth.

'And unable to speak,' I add, erupting into laughter. 'You know how Carlotta loves to talk. It must have been agony for her.'

Ada smiles in spite of herself, pursing her mouth so as not to laugh out loud. I catch my first glimpse of the shy, almost furtive appreciation of other people's unconventional behaviour that lies buried beneath her habitual cautiousness.

'Why does Carlotta go to live in Hobart?' asks Ada. 'Is it because you are there?'

'No. She decided her life in Perth was over and she was attracted to Tasmania. Many artists are. It's a very beautiful place, poetic and melancholy. A strange luminous mist outlines the hills, and painters love this. It's eerie, perfect for romantics like Carlotta — and me, for a while anyway.' Of course it was a bonus that I was there, especially as I was working as director of Hobart's contemporary art space. But Carlotta knew I planned to return to Melbourne.

'Why do you decide to come to Russia?' asks Ada.

'Partly because of Carlotta. We were talking about Hobart, how it's like living on the edge of the world. I'd decided it was time for me to leave, but I didn't want to go back to Melbourne yet. Carlotta suggested "Why don't you go to the other end of the world. Go to Russia."'

Ada laughs. 'This is very typical logic from Carlotta,' she says. 'So, what do you like to do? Of course I show you the many beautiful things in St Petersburg. I take some time away from work because you are coming.'

'That's so good of you, Ada.'

'No, not at all. It is my pleasure to show you. And you

will to meet Tamara and she will take you to places also. So, would you like to meet the artists?'

I hesitate, thinking about this. 'Yes, of course, but not especially artists. I'd like to meet all kinds of people.'

I've spent the past four years with artists. Steeped in art and steeped in the Tasmanian landscape, which is what their art was primarily about: environmental issues, the postmodern sublime, the poetics of darkness and light, melancholy and death. A magnificent landscape; outstanding painters and photographers. It was inspiring to work in such a place with such artists, each one a new world. Shortly before I left I finished writing about and curating an exhibition of their work which was now touring around Australia. I'd immersed myself in it all to saturation level, and that's why it had been time to leave. On to another city, other worlds, perhaps ones that involved more than looking and seeing and interpreting the visual, which has been the focus of my life for too long. Living among strangers in a foreign land will require me to engage with life more directly.

Ada tells me I won't be staying with her in her apartment as arranged. The apartment is only one small room and has no hot water. She has a friend, Dmitri — 'We shorten it to Mitri' — who will move in with her while I stay in his larger apartment. I ask if this arrangement is agreeable to her. We smile at each other knowingly. 'Mitri is quick to take the opportunity to stay with me,' she laughs, amused and resigned.

Mitri is a businessman, she tells me. 'Not high, not low — middle level,' she explains in apologetic tones. 'At first I was not interested. But Mitri is a very delicate man. He does not put the pressure on me. He is kind. Several weeks ago when I was in the hospital, every day he brings me many expensive fruits.'

I recall Carlotta mentioning that Ada has some mysterious gynaecological problem, associated with her having grown up in Tomsk. 'Does Mitri speak English?' I ask.

'A little,' she replies.

———◦•◦———

The train pulls into the centre of the famously flat swampland on the Gulf of Finland that Peter the Great — incongruously to some — selected as the site of Russia's 'window on Europe'. So remote, so damp. It's teeming with rain.

Within seconds a large hand raps on the window. Suddenly Mitri is in our compartment, presenting us with an enormous pink carnation each and swinging my large heavy suitcase off the rack as if it's a sack of feathers. God, I think, here's a member of that endangered species — a real man. Mitri is chunky, earthy, exuberant, delighted to be of service to the ladies, beaming with the joy of it. He has an attractive Slavic face with wide bone structure and thick, longish brown hair, but it's his laughing eyes that make him really appealing. He's rain-drenched.

We emerge into the downpour, umbrella-less. I don't mind: this is early August, late summer in Russia, and it's not cold.

Ada and Mitri are chatting, catching up, and I walk along the platform behind them, watching. Mitri carries my cumbersome suitcase with one hand, disdaining to use its ludicrous pull-strap and wheels, and with the other he gesticulates broadly. His hair and check wool shirt are dripping. Ada, willowy beside him, listens demurely. The rain flattens her hair so that it frames her face sleekly. I appraise her cheap clothes: a floral print dress in thin cotton, oversized khaki jacket in unlined coarse horse-blanket wool (Mitri's), beige vinyl court shoes, beige vinyl handbag with a metal chain. I think of the expensive black clothes Australian curators wear. They wouldn't be caught dead in an image-destroying outfit like Ada's. But nothing can diminish her elegance. Rain drips from my brow and I snuggle into the stylish collar of my second-hand Guilia Minetti over-coat whose orange cashmere sleeve Ada yesterday stroked with a kind of reverence.

Mitri stops and turns, holding out his arm when I catch up to scoop me into the warmth of their friendship.

In Mitri's battered Toyota we drive at breakneck speed through Gogol's city of dreams. Baroque palaces, high clock towers and golden storybook minarets flash by. We arrive at the broad sea-green River Neva. Halfway across one of its arched bridges the traffic, fortuitously, slows down and stops altogether. From this panoramic vantage point I can see how Peter the Great, inspired by the Sun King's Versailles, planned the city as a series of 'prospects', where inhabitants are constantly reminded of its beauty by long vistas. Eighteenth century paintings of these stage-like cities often show gesturing figures, as if daily existence in such settings was alive with dramatic incident.

Mitri rips along the grand embankment that follows the course of the Neva, treating me to a blur of golden imperial eagles atop street lamps. 'There's the Hermitage,' say Ada and Mitri together, indicating the monumental Winter Palace with its white and gold pilastered facade. Enormous, yet weightless as a mirage. 'You go there first on Tuesday,' Ada informs me, referring to the complimentary visits she has lined up for me.

We turn left into legendary Nevsky Prospekt, Nabokov's 'dream-wide street', the arterial causeway central to Peter's extravagant vision. 'Look,' points Ada to a confection of Byzantine arches and jewelled minarets, 'the Cathedral of the Spilled Blood.'

'Why is it called that?' I ask.

'Alexander the Second was assassinated there, blown up by terrorist bomb.'

Amid the elegant classical and art nouveau buildings, with their downstairs shops and cafes, another cathedral of staggering size and pomposity looms into view: St Isaac's. 'Behind there is Dostoevski's apartment,' gestures Ada, as if we might visit him.

'Very bad district,' mutters Mitri.

I remind myself that I'm in the city of Nabokov, Stravinsky, Malevich and the Russian avant-garde, but I'm too travel-dazed to feel excited. How long is it since I've slept?

Thirty-six hours? Forty-eight? I've no idea. Unreal city. Somebody called St Petersburg an unreal city. Who was it? Gogol? Biely? It looks real enough to me. A pink palace with bare-breasted caryatids supporting the upper storey flashes by. How beautiful. It's the fact I'm here that seems unreal. In my imagination there are so many St Petersburgs: Pushkin's 'beauty and marvel' of the north, the imperial city of the Tsars, the revolutionary city of the Bolsheviks, Akhmatova's martyred city under Stalin, the stricken Leningrad of the 900 day siege — all so different. And, I think, excitement breaking through my stupor at last, it's for me to discover the St Petersburg of now.

We drive on. Elegance and baroque flamboyance give way to the architecture of deadly seriousness: the cold art deco of early Stalinism. From 1918 to 1991 St Petersburg was re-named Leningrad, and here it is, Leningrad still. The heavy grey tenement blocks are ornamented with stylised symbols of power: flaming torches, eagle wings, eagle heads, the occasional hammer and sickle.

The landscape shifts again. Now I become alarmed. Towering cube after towering cube. Block after block, neighbourhood after neighbourhood of grubby-green high-rise tenements, all the same. Mile after mile after mile of them, one shabby street indistinguishable from another. The only relief is flat fields of scrubby weeds. I'd resigned myself to the fact that Ada might live in what I've always thought of as commission flats, but Melbourne's housing estates are Manhattan compared to this. The buildings become increasingly squalid, their ugliness reflecting the mind-numbing dullness of utilitarianism, their cell-like structures the view of human beings as mere units of production.

Ada apologises for Mitri's apartment being so far from the centre of the city. By the time we reach his district the facades are actually crumbling. Still determined to regard St Petersburg in poetic terms, I decide we are in Dante's eighth circle of hell.

At the entrance to Mitri's apartment building I recoil. Something stinks. Trash, decay, ancient dust, rotting pipes, leaking sewage. In varying intensities this stench permeates the building and everything in it. It seeps into my clothes, hair and skin. All the Guerlain perfume in the world will not be able to distract from its persistent reek. Before three days are out I'll have used up an entire bottle of Shalimar.

The lift surpasses any nightmare. Normally I'd run off shrieking in terror before stepping into that evil cage. The three of us are pressed together like a moment in the Liverpool soccer disaster. As we clank and shudder upwards my head begins to reel with claustrophobic panic. I fix my eyes firmly on Ada's serene face, only centimetres from mine, and so retain my sanity. That we eventually emerge from that filthy cell will always be one of the miracles of my life. As soon as we do I make them show me where the stairs are. Naturally they're unlit, but for the ninety nights I will spend here I grope my way up and down eight flights of urine-soaked cement stairs in that slimy stairwell, constantly burning my fingers on a cigarette lighter and occasionally dry retching. I never again step into that creaking shuttle to the abyss.

Mitri produces a ring of strangely shaped keys. Each door, Ada explains, has a knack to opening it and Mitri is now going to demonstrate. With balletic precision he manages at the same time to kick the door, heave it with his shoulder and twist the key in the lock with a couple of nifty wrist movements. The pockmarked steel door springs open and we enter the corridor, the building's foul smell hitting me full in the face. Instinctively I grab at my nose. A surly human wreck on an ancient wooden crutch emerges from a door on the right and thuds slowly past us.

Door number two. This, Mitri cheerfully tells me, is the easy one. You must only to be very gentle. He inserts the key slowly, turns it lovingly, and *vot!* steel door number two springs open to reveal steel door number three. The intricacy of thumb and wrist movement, the exquisite coordination of arm and shoulder required to open door number three is achievable only by Mitri. For days, over and over again, he painstakingly seeks to initiate me into the mysteries of this lock. 'Pliz,' he says, 'let us try again.' He takes it very personally that I am never able to master it. He and Ada worry that when I go out I must leave this door unlocked. They tell me it is very dangerous to do this. I promise them I'll bolt it from the inside when I'm in the apartment. Mitri oils all the bolts. There are four of them.

I've prepared myself for the apartment's interior by imagining
the direst scenes of squalor my befuddled brain can conjure.
Once we are indeed inside, I almost weep with relief. Apart from
a toilet that smells like a decomposing corpse and an overwhelming chandelier made from eight carriage lamps — a triumph of
Soviet surrealism — the apartment is almost pleasant. By Russian
standards it's large, with a six-metre-square lounge-cum-
bedroom, a kitchen, a bathroom with a bath, and a sunroom.
The latter is one of those makeshift wooden erections Russians
tack on to the exteriors of tenement blocks, lending them a
certain picturesque quality reminiscent of a Naples slum. The
bathroom has no ventilation, so it stinks of ancient mildew. It
takes five days before the agonies of muscle strain from constant
walking can induce me to soak in that bath. More days pass
before I can sit and read in the sunroom without listening for the
creaking sounds which, I imagine, will signal its collapse.

Throughout the apartment are domestic touches: rugs, a
china cabinet, very clean white lace curtains and a striking
blue textile with an abstract pattern. I later learn this was silk-
screened by Anatole, the Head of Textiles at the St Petersburg
School of Industrial Arts. He and his wife Irina, also a textile
artist, are my neighbours in the next block and the owners of
this apartment. If I have any problems I must go to Anatole,
instructs Ada. 'He doesn't speak the English but he has the
very unusual personality,' she says mystifyingly.

16

'Anatole very bad temper, very funny,' warns Mitri.

'Anatole is a very kind man,' rebukes Ada. Tonight she will take me to Anatole and Irina's apartment so I know how to find them and then they will come back here for dinner.

For now Ada and Mitri leave me to rest, insisting on returning to prepare and eat lunch with me. I am at once deeply touched and mildly panic-stricken by their solicitous attention to my entertainment and wellbeing: apart from ten hours set aside daily for sleep and ablutions, every minute of my first week in St Petersburg is tightly programmed. Before the week is out I come to learn that privacy and solitude — our precious western concepts of personal space — don't really exist in Russia.

Above my bed hangs a large velvet rug depicting bear cubs cavorting in an autumnal forest with mother bear growling protectively in the foreground. Equally Russian is my curious bedcover: a paean to the national talent for inventive make-do. It consists of a coarse double blanket, folded in half, inserted into a central diamond-shaped opening cut into the top sheet of a worn pair sewn together.

It's impossible to sleep. I get up and go to the kitchen window and look out, anticipating an endless monotony of cubes receding into the distance. What I get is far worse — the building next door looming in front of me, blocking the view all the way up to the sky. This to me is hell, particularly after four years of looking out of my window at endless expanses of sea and sky, Hobart nestled at the foot of Mount Wellington in the distance. But I must get used to this, a common enough experience in modern life I tell myself, just as the overall layout of St Petersburg is common to many European cities: an exquisite decaying historical centre ringed by stupefyingly ugly twentieth century high-rises.

I go back to bed and try to sleep, lying there thinking. The singular fact we all remember about St Petersburg is that it was founded by a tyrant; less well known but equally obvious once you're here is that its outskirts were built during the reign of another tyrant. No other great city I can think of is so clearly associated with — and physically demarcated by — two tyrants, two epochs. St Petersburg is also the stage of a curious reversal: it's not the historical centre that's decaying but its modern periphery. It's as if the city remembers Peter the Great as a builder and Stalin as a destroyer.

Features of cities can be metaphors for the minds of the people who shaped them. The differences between the St Petersburgs of Peter the Great and Stalin show the contrasting world views of two tyrants. Peter's broad prospects with their vistas stretching into infinity symbolise hope and possibility. Even the city's most wretched inhabitant could be soothed by its beauty, awed by its grandeur, inspired to thoughts of liberation by its expansiveness. Such thoughts probably played a subliminal role in inspiring the Bolsheviks to revolution. It's ironic that the chief inheritor of that revolution, Stalin, created the very opposite of a liberating environment — spaces of psychological entrapment. The buildings around me are designed to dull the mind with standardisation and end-less repetition, to block the view. It's a way of life with no prospects.

It's not until Ada and Mitri return, eat lunch with me and leave again, that I finally fall into a deep sleep.

I awake several hours later to a wet sensation on my nose. I open my eyes to a tiny black and white kitten sitting on my neck, sniffing my face. Above it is Ada, smiling. 'You must to get up now. Anatole and Irina will come soon.'

'Is this yours?' I ask, yawning deeply and lifting the little kitten in the air.

'This small cat Mitri has rescued last week. I will tell you his story afterwards. Come on, you must to get up,' she says, pulling the covers off.

'I find this cat for Ada,' yells Mitri from the kitchen. 'It has no name and you must help us.'

'It's a baby cat, Mitri, a kitten. Say kitten,' I yell back.

'Kit-ten, kit-ten.'

When our visitors arrive I see immediately what Mitri means about Anatole. '*Zdravstvuite*,' I say to him and Irina, having rehearsed the Russian word for 'hello' with Ada before they arrive. Neither of them speaks English.

Anatole guffaws. '*Zdravstvuite*,' he mimics in a mock-feminine squeak. What a bastard, I think. I curl my lip at him snarlingly. He curls his back at me and growls and his exaggerated expression makes me laugh. Thus begins our unusual relationship.

Irina gives him a whack on the arm and, delivering a smiling speech in Russian, presents me with a bunch of red and yellow chrysanthemums.

'Irina say you are very welcome to St Petersburg and she hope you have most wonderful time in our so special city,' says Ada. 'You must go to her and Anatole if you need the help and she is very sorry she doesn't speak the English.'

'Tell her I'm very sorry I don't speak Russian,' I say, kissing Irina on her soft cheek. She's very feminine, pretty in an old-fashioned way with bouffant blonde curls and start-lingly blue eyes, but with good Russian bone structure like her husband. Anatole looks like a character Gogol might have invented — I will come to learn he behaves like one too. He's quite handsome in a devilish way, brown hair hugging his head like a Roman sculpture and glittering hazel eyes which he narrows in a mock scowl. His big brush of a moustache would look ridiculous on most men, but it suits him. What a charis-matic couple they are.

The evening passes in a blur; I'm stupefied with sleepiness and long to go back to bed. 'How is Carlotta?' they want to know. They're delighted with her and my Australian presents — French perfume, lingerie, cosmetics, books of Aboriginal art, good liquor and other luxuries that are impossible to find in Russia or too expensive.

The kitten settles on Anatole's lap. 'You must tell us name for this kit-ten,' says Mitri, demolishing a bottle of brandy with Anatole while Irina sketches us all.

The kitten's a classic black and white. 'Felix,' I say immediately.

They love this because it's a Russian name. I tell them the story of Felix the cartoon cat and teach them to sing the song: 'Felix the cat, the wonderful, wonderful cat'.

———•·•———

Two weeks later I'm alone, I have no idea where I am, I've been wandering around lost for close to an hour, the streets are deserted except for suspicious-looking characters — one of whom seems to be following me — and it's getting darker by the minute.

I'm furious with myself. I was anxious to get home after an interminable afternoon waiting with Ada in queues to have my visa stamped, so, after some food shopping, I took a risk and caught a trolleybus numbered 22a. My bus is 22, I'd never seen a 22a before, so I assumed the *a* was a mistake and it would follow the 22 route. It did until it reached the middle of the high-rise wasteland, but then it must have veered off somewhere, impossible to know where exactly because all the buildings and streets look the same — are the same. It's difficult enough to find my stop on the right bus; I have to watch vigilantly for an identifying supermarket on a far corner of the block. It was only when, stop after stop, this supermarket didn't appear that I knew I was in the wrong neighbourhood, even though it looked exactly the same as Mitri's.

That's the problem. Any of the tenement blocks looming around me could be Mitri's and as it gets darker the subtle distinguishing feature that belongs to his block alone — the scratched blue door to the stairs — is becoming increasingly difficult to identify.

My search has been systematic. I'm working my way in snakelike curves past all the buildings on the west side of what I'm pretty sure is the main thoroughfare to St Petersburg. I've now done two blocks, searched around forty buildings for the blue door. It's only logical that I must eventually find it. So I tell myself, well aware that my cool retreat into method is to prevent me from screaming my head off. Wandering around in all this menacing sameness searching for a minor difference feels like the onset of madness.

It's time to ask a passer-by for assistance, even if it does have to be a suspicious-looking character. What choice do I have?

No one here speaks English, but luckily, in a little book I always carry with me, I've jotted down vital information like Mitri's address and Ada's address and telephone number. Beside each, Ada has written the Russian in Cyrillic script. I've also listed useful Russian phrases I refer to for shopping and getting around; I've no ear for Russian and remember none of it. All I have to do now is memorise some basic words and point to Mitri's address in the book.

I put the shopping down and rummage in my handbag, thinking the least a passer-by can do is point me in the right direction. Considering how helpful Russians can be, I'll probably be escorted to my door. Naturally the book doesn't immediately present itself. I wonder where it's safer to search the bag more thoroughly — in plain view or in the shadow of a doorway? I stay where I am. I place the contents of my handbag one by one into the shopping bag until — oh god, please, no — the handbag is empty. I don't have the little book!

Frantically I search the shopping bag and my coat pockets. Inconceivable as it is, I must have left the book behind this morning. I picture it on the kitchen table, its soft green cover. Now I'm cut off from my only means of asking for assistance. I don't even know my own address, or Ada's. Even if there was a taxi on these godforsaken streets, I'd be unable to give the driver directions.

My head feels tight and I'm exhausted. I'm approaching the middle of one of the estates and ahead of me is a rubbish-strewn open area. I must cross this to reach the tenements on the other side. The thought of walking into that darkness followed by the shadowy figure fills me with panic. It will take at least five minutes to walk from here to there. On impulse I decide to make a run for it, full pelt. I drop my shopping bag, then change my mind. I stand stock-still, staring at the uneven ground with its untidy protrusions of junk. To run across there without tripping is impossible; I'd almost certainly break a leg.

I can't stand it any longer. It's face my fears or die. Before I can change my mind, I turn abruptly and walk purposefully toward my follower with some vague plan to slap his face and catch him off guard.

There's nobody there. He's gone, trailed into some building long ago probably.

I look all around me. Not a figure in sight. I look up. This, I think, trying to buck myself up with metaphysics, a narrative — anything — is the great existential moment of my life. Just me and the night sky. A bird, I zoom up into the dark blue sky and picture looking down on myself from high above, a human ant surrounded by towering bunkers of thousands of people behind steel doors and lighted windows, people I can't access — the quintessential modernist experience.

Something has emerged from one of the rubbish heaps and is moving toward me. The knot in my stomach releases some kind of acid and nausea rises all the way up to my throat, but I'm only half aware of this; my head seems to be floating even though all my concentration is riveted on the approaching figure. From miles away, I wonder if I'm in shock.

The form moves into the light. I see it's a comfortingly dumpy old woman in a paisley headscarf who's been gathering scrap wood. I walk toward her with an emotion approaching joy and utter the one Russian phrase I can remember: '*Golye muzey?*' She looks up at my face from under her thick eyebrows, studying it to work out whether I'm dangerous or merely demented. I've just asked her, 'Where is the museum?'

I repeat the phrase, gesturing to indicate how utterly lost I am. She speaks in Russian and I speak in English with gestures and soon this sharp-eyed babushka understands. She takes my shopping bag, deposits half of her wood in it and returns it to me, and with one hand now free, she takes my hand firmly in hers and leads me to a nearby tenement.

Minutes later we're in her living room and she's plying me with tea, vodka and salted cucumbers while she barks orders at three men and two women who've gathered in a circle to stare at me in amazement. Eventually two of the men leave.

My face is beginning to hurt from smiling at this generous woman, whose name is Lena. A sense of the awkwardness of the situation is taking over from my relief at being rescued from the night. I can see that at least four people sleep in this room and I know that Lena will absolutely insist on providing me with a comfortable bed for the night and probably deprive one of her children or grandchildren — or even herself — of theirs. I've been in enough Russian homes now to know that what little they have is shared and a guest — even a stranger — always comes first.

I'm making signs to convey that I'm happy to spend the night in the armchair. The front door opens noisily and I hear hilarity in the hallway. The two men have returned with a third. The three of them come into the room and I stare at the craggy face with the thick moustache, the dancing eyes and demonic grin, and I can't believe it. Anatole! He stands over me, frowning with pursed lips, waving a pointed finger in my face: Naughty naughty naughty girl — what have you been up to this time? (This is how we communicate.) I'm shrieking with joyful surprise. He stands on tiptoe and with mincing little ballet steps, waving his arms undulatingly, he repeats,

'*Golye muzey? Golye muzey?*' in a mocking effeminate voice. They must have told him how Lena found me. Tears of laughter stream down my face. I hear the word 'Arfstraalian' in their conversation and realise Lena knew of my connection with Anatole because word had travelled that an Australian visitor was actually living in the neighbourhood.

Anatole and I walk back to our estate. It's only a block away but to the east of the main road, not the west. I'd never have found it.

THE ENCHANTED FOREST

———◆———

The story goes like this. Once upon a time in a faraway kingdom an ailing prince lived in a magical house in an enchanted forest. The prince, who never married, had travelled to many distant lands and delighted in games, codes and ciphers. The magical house had towering columns, many many light-filled rooms, as many dark corners, and a secret staircase. It stood high on a hill, near a bridge that crossed a wide winding river. The surrounding enchanted forest was a summer kingdom of warm lakes and bright mushrooms, of wild apple trees, lupins and columbines. The forest floor was a carpet of soft grass and curative herbs. Gorgeous butterflies flitted among its lime trees and whispering pines. Perhaps then there were the sounds of birds and animals — bears and elks maybe. I do not know, for now this place is silent.

The old prince died and passed on his kingdom to the young prince, his nephew. Here the young prince spent his mornings chasing butterflies, his afternoons absorbing the chiaroscuro ambience of the house, and his evenings writing poetry about this place, its paradoxes, its many illusions and tricks of light.

The young prince was very handsome. Sometimes, with the gold coins he had inherited from the old prince in his pocket, he would go to the glittering nearby city to attend parties and balls and net the beautiful butterflies of the night. No one was, had been or would ever be as happy as the young prince.

Disaster struck swiftly. Overnight the old order toppled and the young prince was forced to flee. He travelled to many foreign lands, settling here and there, unsettled, until finally, when he reached the New World, he accepted his fate and became just that — a traveller, always a traveller.

Never again could he return to his enchanted kingdom, but everywhere, always, he carried it with him. To soothe himself he would conjure up its enchantments: its butterflies, its dappled light, its dark hidden staircase and the echoing voices of its velvet rooms. The prince so enchanted others with his conjurings that eventually he became a magician, some say the greatest magician of his time.

In old age, when his magic had made him wealthy once again, he returned to the Old World (not his old world) and lived high among snowy peaks to be nearer to his beloved kingdom, forever lost, forever with him.

I stand before Rozhestveno, the magical house. We'd been driving through the countryside for over an hour, on our way to Irina's dacha a few kilometres away. I was so taken by a beautiful church with royal-blue onion domes that I failed to notice the house on its distant hill, across the winding Oredezh River. It is in any case almost obscured by tall trees. Ada shouted at Mitri to stop and turned to me excitedly. 'I have something to show you.'

Mitri waits in the car, Felix the kitten sitting on his shoulder, while we stand here and gape.

I've seen this house before, in a winter photograph. In this it stands tall, three storeys, in a stark landscape of white snow and leafless black trees, its four monumental ionic columns and its many windows and shuttered French doors white, its horizontal timbers grey. Snow-covered wooden steps lead up to the columned portico.

Standing here, to my surprise, I discover that the columns, which look like white stone in the photograph, must have been timber — towering tree trunks capped by delicately carved ionic scrolls. Nothing could be more Russian, this combination of classical architecture and vernacular timbers.

Rozhestveno was designed in the eighteenth century by Rastrelli, the architect of the Imperial Winter Palace (now the Hermitage). The magical house in its surrounding forest was indeed an enchanted place. It survived the Revolution and seven decades of Soviet dictatorship. For the duration of Vladimir Nabokov's sixty year life of exile the house he inherited when he was prince of this kingdom remained as it was, silent and deserted in the whispering forest, as if Nabokov's art had cast a spell on it.

In the 1980s it served as a museum of the Siversky region. It was the one place in all Russia that displayed a few of the banned Nabokov's works: affectionately sentimental early poems about the surrounding countryside and the Oredezh River. The European and American works of Nabokov's maturity were, of course, never referred to. Even now many Russians cannot come to terms with *Lolita*.

Nabokov's spell lingered on after his death; then the sleeping house was finally awakened to time present.

The mysterious fire which all but destroyed Rozhestveno occurred only a few years ago. Now the magical house is a Constructivist assemblage of one standing ionic column, charred black timbers, and the raw yellow of recent scaffolding. The latter implies a determination to hold it all together, and even suggests that one day the Russians, masters of reconstruction, may reconstruct Rozhestveno. But, for the time being, the house is abandoned, a blackened ruin all but hidden amidst the shimmering foliage of its still enchanted forest.

From one side of the house you can ascend earth-covered steps and enter the blackened interior through a grand double door. Curiously, it still feels like a wonderful house. In the nobly proportioned entrance, I glimpse a staircase going off at a strange angle. I have the sense that the house is, not exactly familiar, but 'the way it should be'.

I balance my way across the charred floor joists with some vague ambition of finding the secret staircase Tsarevich Alexei Mikhailovich (son of Catherine the Great and Rozhestveno's first owner) had built for secret assignations and escapes. Ada hovers by the entrance door, edgy, afraid something may collapse. It seems solid enough to me; no threatening creaks. The absolute silence seems benign. I enter a large dim high-ceilinged room, its walls a lacework of barely moving shadows. The foliage outside casts these baroque forms. I stand still. Then I experience that rush, that heightened sense of being an intruder in time past, which is a kind of ecstasy to me. And now I know why this house is wonderful: it's the quality of the light, a dark velvet gloom, tinged warm brown — the night side of chiaroscuro: mysterious, pervasive, impenetrable. I'm enveloped in another century.

This reminds me of Nabokov's Uncle Ruka, from whom he inherited this house and who is said to have 'dwelt in a golden past'. I'm fond of Ruka, or Vasily Ivanovich Rukavishnikov, as a biographical figure because of the contradictions in his character. He was, during the reign of Tsar Alexander III, ambassador to the Russian Imperial Embassy in Rome. Aristocratic, insouciant and eccentric, Ruka lived in the grand manner, travelled widely — to America even — and amused himself by translating passages of literature into ciphers, including Hamlet's most famous speech. His perilous health, his homosexuality, his tendency to reminisce about his past, and his love of secret codes and word games led his nephew to describe him as Proustian. The peasants on Ruka's estate had a far less romantic epithet for him; they nicknamed him 'the bottom feeler', for Ruka liked little boys. Nabokov was silent about this, though some think that Ruka's sexual decadence and love of puzzles was the inspiration for Clare Quilty, Humbert's nemesis in *Lolita*.

Behind a charcoaled mess that may have been bookshelves there is a spiral staircase, narrow and enclosed. I begin the winding ascent which, on the third turn, leads Piranesi-like to … nothing. Nowhere or heaven, depending on how you look at it. Fresh air, open sky. Fire has devoured this upper section of the house. Nabokov might have liked the idea of his legendary staircase leading nowhere. But I can't know if my easy discovery is the secret staircase; who now would know? I suspect it isn't, that the real one is still hidden away between walls of the ruin which are too dangerous for trespass.

It's getting dark. We leave and drive on into the enchanted forest, the harvest moon 'against' the sky, as the Russians say. Before the Revolution Nabokov's mother's family, the Rukavishnikovs, owned all this land. At the beginning of every summer, as soon as the Nabokovs arrived here from town, she would get down on her hands and knees and kiss the earth.

———•·•———

Irina's dacha is charming, a typically Russian wooden summer cottage, its shutters and facia boards picturesquely carved, set in a garden in a street of similar variously coloured ones. Irina's is cadmium yellow. The other streets — winding country dirt lanes with large peppercorn and fir trees — are in turn similar and form a village reminiscent of ones described a century ago by Chekhov or Turgenev.

Dachas have a holiday feel; they're for summer habitation only, their lack of heating and plumbing making then virtually uninhabitable in the winter. I'm surprised they still exist; I'd assumed the Bolsheviks had abolished all private property, but Ada tells me Irina inherited this one from her uncle, so perhaps dachas, such a traditional feature of Russian life, were an exception. I come to learn that educated Russians, even the many in penurious circumstances, spend part of the summer at a dacha, a friend's or a rented one — the rents are minimal.

Irina has had to stay in town to organise an exhibition of textiles at the St Petersburg School of Art. I am both disappointed and relieved at this news. As soon as I met Irina I felt drawn to her warm personality; we clearly like each other and might be friends but for the fact that we have no means of communicating. Irina is highly energetic, one of those people who is never still, and she's impatient with translated conversations. Each time we meet, after kisses on the cheek in greeting, we constantly nod and smile at one another, which, after a few minutes, becomes a strain. This is the price I pay for not speaking Russian.

I manage to communicate with Anatole on some strange level through exaggerated expressions and gestures — a kind of dual comedy act which makes Ada and Mitri laugh. There's a Harpo Marx kind of anarchy to Anatole's personality, a curious blend of arrogance and clownishness, that something in me responds to. And he is, as Ada insisted on my first day here, extraordinarily generous.

He's standing in the driveway, waiting for us with a mock ceremonial welcome.

We enter a wide room, summery, comfortable and artlessly attractive, to the right a kitchen with large red and green lead-light windows. Immediately I sense Irina, her casual stylishness. A rustic ladder leads up to a trapdoor and I'm intrigued as to

what's beyond. Brandishing a torch, Anatole leads me up there. We bend our heads as we walk along a low-roofed corridor carpeted with wood shavings. By torchlight we emerge into a storybook attic bedroom, cosy and secluded, with fresh pine walls and a counterpane knitted in rainbow colours. I beg to be allowed to sleep here but Anatole pretends to forbid me because he hasn't yet completed it.

We're tired from the journey, so after a hasty dinner of tinned meat, potatoes, cucumber and vodka, we prepare for bed. Anatole clutches his head theatrically and shakes his fist at me as I make my way back up the sturdy ladder with a torch. I switch it off as soon as I reach the high room with its pine smell, its chaste bed set between a steeply slanting wall and large stained-glass window. All of this is illuminated yellow by the moon.

I don't sleep well (the vodka, the coffee). I wake at five. It's cold in the attic. I watch as it gradually grows light behind the dark silhouetted trees, my mind a collage of fragments from three weeks in St Petersburg. The excited face of an elderly Jewish artist preparing for his first exhibition in New York, his cramped studio stacked with expressive portraits of St Petersburg — its bridges and streets in the snow, the sun, the night. The European paintings in the Hermitage — the heavenly blue of Leonardo's Madonna Litta — and the Russian ones in the Russian Museum — the inky blue of the dress, the cubist shawl, in Altman's mannerist portrait of the poet Anna Akhmatova. The theatrical opulence of the marble staircases stormed by the Bolsheviks at the Hermitage — what a setting for a revolution's opening night. Art and history and art and more history and art. Ada and I love them; this common ground is why we clicked almost immediately. In my mind's collage Ada is the central image, her face and graceful form and the graciousness with which she has taken on the role of my host in St Petersburg. I picture her direct gaze. Friends in Australia tell me that I sometimes speak my mind too directly, that I can be direct to the point of rudeness. Ada is the same. I find this an immense relief.

A few days ago, just before Ada introduced me to Tamara, her colleague at the museum with whom she's very close, she said to me, 'Tamara is very intelligent woman and you must be serious.' 'Aren't I always?' I asked, a bit mystified. 'No, sometimes you make the joke and you must not when you first meet Tamara,' she replied instructively. We were standing outside the Russian Museum waiting for Tamara beneath the bronze statue of Pushkin, which was apt because when she finally arrived Tamara reminded me of Pushkin's Tatiana at the ball: dignified and remote, long-suppressed passions behind her eyes. The three of us walked across the road to the vast Shostakovich Hall where, seated on red velvet armchairs under pendulous chandeliers that shimmered like diamonds, we listened to a concert performed as part of the international festival of barbershop quartets. The experience was for me surreal, especially when an American quartet called the Gashouse Gang performed to the opening tune of Beethoven's

Fifth Symphony, a song with the opening lines, 'We're four short guys/ who like to harmonise'.

I made no comment, was serious as instructed, and was later rewarded by Ada telling me that Tamara would like me to accompany her to the Peterhof Palace the next morning.

———•·•———

I get up at six, quietly, so as not to disturb the others. I go down the path to the country toilet and endure its foul miasmas, then make myself a cup of tea and take it back outside, sipping it as I stroll among the white daisies offset by paprika nasturtiums, the tall deep-lavender high-heeled shoes speckled white, and the laden apple trees and bilberries at the back. In the pink dawn I photograph the dacha's decorative timber fretwork and its spreading plum tree, pick some columbines and put them in a vase on the kitchen table, and go back to bed, so tired that I soon fall asleep to the sound of Mitri's thunderous snoring.

Ada wakes me at 7.30. 'Wake up, my darling,' she calls as she mounts the ladder. 'This small terrible cat kept me awake all night,' she says, holding Felix aloft and gently shaking him.

We sit in the kitchen and sip tea, red and green sunlight streaming through the windows. Anatole staggers in and sits at the table, clutching his head and groaning, his craggy-handsome face grumpy.

Anatole and I begin one of our conversations, punctuated with dumb-show gestures and noisy exclamations, where he speaks Russian and I English and we seem to understand each other nevertheless.

He likes the word 'hangover' and explores the feel of it with his favourite mock-foreign accent, German: 'Han-gover, han-gover,' he repeats gutturally, his sensuous lips forming a mock snarl.

Mitri is still snoring.

———•·•———

There's a scuffling at the door. It's pushed open and in walks a short, gnarled man with a benevolent smile bearing a turquoise plastic bowl of berries. A strange wrinkled brown dog rushes in past him.

'Viktor!' Ada jumps up excitedly and Anatole blows him a kiss. Ada tells me he's the next-door neighbour and Anatole's brother-in-law and he wishes to speak with me.

Viktor approaches me, places the bowl of berries reverentially in front of me and, bowing, delivers a ceremonial speech.

I don't understand a word but gather that he's welcoming me. He appears to have met very few, if any, non-Russians. He exudes such goodwill that I spontaneously take his hand. He's delighted.

Ada and I head off with Viktor to go mushrooming. We go through the back gate and pass a well where a young couple is doing their washing. Ada tells me Irina's grandfather built this well, which is fed by a natural spring, and now the whole village uses it.

The forest comes right up to the village and soon we're walking in the silence beneath tall black pines and white birches. The forest floor is littered with pine cones. There are wild strawberries, Queen Anne's lace, and herbs in bright green, blue-green or furry silver clumps. Ada tells me most of the herbs are medicinal and that Viktor knows the properties of them all.

We go deeper into the forest and I find the first mushroom, a bright yellow one.

The young Nabokov chased butterflies here. Four or five hours every summer morning. I half close my eyes and imagine him darting across the carpet of soft grass, zigzagging between the tall pines, net raised in pursuit of flitting variegated wings. But there are no butterflies here any more. Perhaps he caught them all. There are plenty of his mother's well-loved mushrooms though, bright orange ones, magical speckled red ones and brown family clusters scattered all over the forest floor.

We descend a steep gully. Ada goes first and, turning, stretches out her hand to help me down. I am struck by the image of her beautiful upturned face framed by her ash-blonde bob, her green eyes smiling into mine. How aristocratic she is, I think, and before I know what I'm saying I ask her, 'Do you think you'll end up married to Mitri?'

'This is a question I must ask myself,' she replies.

'You don't love him, do you?'

'No,' she replies without hesitating. 'Only as the friend.'

'Is it because he's not your equal, I mean in education?' I ask as we walk side by side across an open field surrounded by trees, Viktor leading the way.

'No. Slava and my first husband were very educated but not kind to me like Mitri.'

'You had another husband before Slava?' I ask, surprised.

'Yes. A poet I marry in Tomsk.'

'What happened to him?'

'I must tell you some other time,' she says quietly. 'It is a very bad story.'

We go on chatting as the three of us meander between clusters of mushrooms, stooping to fill our buckets, twigs crackling beneath our feet.

Ada returns to the house to prepare the mushrooms for lunch and Viktor takes me back a different way along a high embankment where wild apple trees grow, their branches heavy with clusters of green fruit. Occasionally he bends down and picks leaves from various herbs.

We return to the aroma of the mushroom omelettes Ada has prepared for lunch. On the floor are buckets of yellow and brown mushrooms soaking in brine. Mitri comes in with cucumbers from the garden. He slices them into four and puts them on a large plate with wild dill and a bowl of salt. We eat.

I'm curious about Viktor's folkloric knowledge of herbs so, through Ada, he tells me this.

'My grandmother was an uneducated woman but she possessed two old medical books and a microscope that she used regularly. She made many different medicines from herbs but her most famous one was made from snake venom. Her instruments were a pronged stick and a piece of glass. She tapped the snake on either side of the head with the points of the stick. This caused it to spew its venom onto the glass. Then she would put the venom in a phial.'

'What did she use this medicine for?' I ask.

Viktor looks uncomfortable but Ada, increasingly fascinated, encourages him. Eventually she turns to me. 'She make the baby go away.'

'Did many women go to her?' I ask.

'Many women. Many too from St Petersburg.'

'Was this before or after the Revolution?'

'Both. The Revolution doesn't change anything for her because she is close to the nature. She crazy, they think, so they don't bother with her. The Soviets, not many come here anyway.'

We walk along a track to the lake; Anatole gives me his hand when we come to slippery dips and rises. We arrive at a serene landscape — a wide blue lake encircled with pines expanding beyond a grassy embankment where we sit. It's hot, which is strange because I'd always imagined northern Russia as eternally cold.

I approach the water, the soft sandy soil pleasant beneath my feet. The water mixes with the soil as I walk in and becomes murky. To my surprise the lake isn't cold. Ada and Mitri join me, Mitri passing me as he wades out. Anatole sits hugging his knees on the shore, still grumpy-faced.

Mitri turns and tells Ada to go back. The water is too cold for her after her operation. Ada's 'women's problems', as she describes them, have required more than one operation, but she has only mentioned this to me once, on the train from Moscow. Her manner was so reserved that I've never referred to the subject, so it surprises me to hear Mitri refer to it publicly like this, so loudly and in English.

I plunge under the water, breaststroking forward with elation. For the first time in my life I'm swimming in a lake and it's in Russia! I re-emerge, laughing.

Mitri yells something and swims toward me, disappearing under the water where I've just been swimming.

'The river has taken your sunglasses,' yells Ada from the shore.

Mitri continues diving for them. I tell him to stop — I never liked them anyway.

He wades toward me, shaking his finger in a mock reprimand. 'Think before you swim,' he enunciates slowly. Ada and I squeal with delight at his sudden mastery of English.

When I return to the shore, Anatole becomes agitated and returns to the house.

'What's the matter with him?' I ask.

'He think maybe you get the sunburn in these small clothes you wear,' says Ada, eyeing my dripping shorts. 'He bring you some clothes of Irina.'

Anatole returns with a blue tiered peasant skirt with a lace-up waist and a red-splotched yellow T-shirt.

'Anatole tell you he bought the T-shirt in Scotland and it matches your hair,' says Ada.

I go into the forest, change behind a bush and re-emerge to yips of approval.

'Now you are Russian woman, Anatole tell you,' says Ada.

Anatole grabs my shoulders. 'You Vika,' he shouts.

Now they call me Vika, which seems as natural to me as

my real name. I could interpret this in a romantic light, that I was a Russian in another life, as Carlotta insists we both were, but really it's the informality of the name that appeals, its tacit invitation to relax with all of them and be a Russian in this life — for a while anyway.

After an afternoon nap we sit outside in the warm night air eating chicken shaslik, potato salad, bread and a bowl of delicious forest mushrooms and onions Viktor cooked and brought over. We're drinking vodka and kvas. At least I'm drinking kvas, a drink made out of fermented rye bread. Ada tells me I like it because characters in nineteenth century Russian novels are always drinking it. She's right, but I like its mellow taste anyway.

They ply me with vodka and we toast everything from Australia and Pushkin to Viktor's strange wrinkled dog Riff, who they tell me is a Chinese shar-pei. We become exuberant, raucous, although Ada looks a little strained. How exhausting it must be for her, I think, translating for me all the time, so I turn to Anatole to find that our understanding is boosted considerably by our vodka intake. Our conversation becomes so uproarious that I grab his face in both my hands and give him a smacking kiss on the cheek. This provokes loud exclamations around the table, playfully exaggerated oohs and ahs; their disapproval, I sense, is real nevertheless. Anatole seems delighted with this chaotic moment.

'Australians do this, kiss each other on the cheek,' I feel compelled to explain. 'It doesn't mean anything. It's friendship.'

Ada doesn't look too convinced. 'Viktor wants to ask you something,' she says.

I turn to Viktor sitting next to me to find him staring up at me with awestruck adoration — I am that rare and exotic creature, a foreign visitor.

'He wants to know if your husband in Australia is a good man.'

'You know I'm not married. Tell him.'

'Why?' asks Mitri mournfully. 'Why you not have the husband?'

'Vy? Vy?' intones Anatole, thumping the table and giggling drunkenly.

I tell them that in Australia women are equal with men and sometimes don't need husbands. Occasionally the man stays at home and looks after the child while the woman works. Ada translates.

Mitri and Viktor look appalled. Anatole's too drunk to care. He keeps interrupting the conversation, talking ceaselessly, so I put my hand over his mouth to shut him up and they laugh. He goes on talking anyway.

'Anatole say you have no respect for him,' says Ada, smiling at last.

Mitri stands up importantly. A pronouncement is imminent. 'Vika,' he says, looking at me from the other side of the table, swaying only slightly. 'I … LOVE … ADA.'

45

I tell him I know this — it's obvious — and he's delighted. He walks around to my side of the table, squeezing in between Anatole and me.

Anatole stands up and angrily challenges him to a duel. We ignore him.

'Mitri wishes to tell you his problems,' says Ada.

'You must try to tell me in English,' I say to Mitri. 'Ada is too tired to translate.'

'No, please, I am happy to translate,' says Ada. 'I am most interested to know what Mitri thinks are his problems.'

They begin.

'Before the Revolution Mitri's family were landowners. They mattered in the society; they had a place. His father is a technician for satellites who knows all the works of Pushkin and Dostoevski. He lived in St Petersburg during the war and survived the Siege of Leningrad. Over one million people die of starvation in the siege. Is like miracle that Vassily, Mitri's father, survive. So his father is part of history. But Mitri will never be this. He has not the land and has not the education.' It hasn't occurred to me that Mitri feels dispossessed, rankled by his situation in life. I wonder if he's become more so recently, now that he's with Ada and her well-educated circle of friends. Indeed Ada is devoted to scholarship and is currently studying German. Mitri speaks passionately, welcoming the opportunity to unburden himself of thoughts that I suspect are as much part of him as his customary cheerfulness. 'Russia ... nobody knows what it is any more. Mitri is afraid his business will be taken away from him.'

'What exactly is his business?' I ask.

'He has two shops selling oil.'

'And he brings the oil from Moscow?'

'Yes.'

'Who'll take the business away?' I ask.

Ada shrugs, so I don't pursue it. She uses the term 'mafia' with me privately, but never in company.

I embark on a half-drunken monologue about the failure of socialism and communism — the bright hopes of the twentieth century destroyed by tyrants and madmen. 'Now Australians too have nothing,' I wail. 'No beliefs, no ideologies.'

'We must believe in God,' shouts Mitri in English, sounding so like a Brother Karamazov I can hardly believe my ears. So much for the Bolsheviks stamping out religion.

Near midnight, after coffee, we leave Mitri and Anatole to their conversation in the kitchen and Viktor leads Ada and me on a night walk through the forest. We walk beneath overhanging trees along a path shining white in the moonlight. It's warm — blood temperature. The path becomes flattened grass. Nature is gentle beneath our feet, sweet-smelling and caressing.

Viktor gives me his hand down the steep gullies. Although he's a stranger and I'm not physically drawn to him, this doesn't feel uncomfortable.

We go on through the forest. The trees enclose us, but the grassy path is clear.

After some time we come to the river flat. The water shines silver in the moonlight. I feel elated, which might be partly due to the vodka.

Victor says if I want to take off my clothes to swim, he'll look the other way. I do.

It's heavenly, the warm water in the night and the yellow moon above, the distant protective frame of trees. I swim in the soft water and hear my own splashing in the silence. A swim in a river in Russia in the moonlight. The chattering in my head ceases. I am for once serene.

Ada stands on the bank with my clothes. I dress and we walk back through the warm silence.

I stop to listen to the night landscape and the whisper of the trees, the wind softly rippling through the leaves. Whishsh.

The earth is astonishingly smooth beneath my bare feet — the unfamiliarity of no twigs or stones underfoot, the absence of pain or discomfort. Everything in the forest is softly silhouetted, its forms as I pass through them a moonlight embrace. Never before have I experienced nature as benign like this. Beautiful as the Australian landscape can be, I am always aware of myself as an intruder there, whereas to be here is to step back into the familiar forests of childhood fairytales. As we wander along I think how strange it is that I should feel more at home in a Russian forest than in the Australian bush, a landscape which — even more curious — I've experienced and considered at length in my writings on Australian artists. I wonder if this is because I'm a city dweller and think of it more in terms of a spectacle than a place to be myself in.

Viktor points at some bushes and turns to us excitedly.

'Viktor tell us that last year, just a few months ago, he see a bear in this place.'

'A big Russian bear?'

'Yes, a brown bear.' Her voice quietens. 'But I don't believe him.'

'Why not? Viktor wouldn't lie about things he saw in the forest, would he?'

'No, he doesn't make the lie, but always he want to see the bear, so he see it.'

'Why do you think it's not true? Are bears nearly extinct in Russia?'

She shrugs. The concept of extinction of species is unfamiliar to most Russians. Even though, like Viktor, I hope bears still roam this forest, I cannot imagine anything menacing lurking in this landscape — unlike the sense I always have in the Australian bush at night. There is nothing frightening here, I say to myself, nearly ecstatic. Only the trees, the soft ground, the warm breeze and my benevolent companions. No wonder they call it Mother Russia.

Yet Stalin loathed the natural world. Like everything else in Soviet Russia, nature had to be pressed into servitude or eradicated. Even that wasn't enough. It was the relationship between man and nature that Stalin despised. How else to explain what is perhaps the most incomprehensible of all his maniacal edicts? At a time when the majority of the country was on the brink of starvation, he forbad ordinary Russians to grow their own fruit and vegetables. Cabbage patches, lemon trees, cucumbers became outlawed. This must have driven Russians crazy because they love growing food.

Paying calls on Anatole's friends in the village next morning, every dacha we pass has its vegetable garden — cabbages, pumpkin, onions, capsicums, beets, cucumber — its grape and berry vines and fruit trees. Two white goats, mythological-looking creatures, tug at bright green grass that slopes down to the lake. A toothless old woman in scarf and gumboots looks up from tying her beans as we pass. I think of this old woman being arrested by the KGB for doing this and burst out laughing.

Ada asks me what I find so funny and I tell her. She frowns deeply. There are certain things Russians cannot ever laugh at. I apologise and explain that my laughter is hysteria at the thought of some cretin telling me I can't grow a cabbage.

———•◦•———

In the evening, on the way back to St Petersburg, we stop once again at Rozhestveno. I look down at the river, orange in the sunset, with its black trees. It occurs to me that the stone bridge crossing the Oredezh is, of course, the one Nabokov writes of in *Speak, Memory*, the one he rode his bicycle to on summer nights to meet his adorable Tamara. The very ground beneath my feet is where he once picked dahlias for Tamara; it formed part of Uncle Ruka's 'huge, dense, two-century-old park with its classical cripples of green-stained stone … and labyrinthine paths radiating from a central fountain'. Only Nabokov would refer to (armless? legless?) classical statues as cripples.

Pocketing an acorn and tiny pine cone, I notice a gnarled old tree near the river and pick its red fruits, mistaking them for crab apples.

Back in St Petersburg, the kitchen resembles a seventeenth century Dutch still life. Ada laughs as I make an arrangement on the table like a *vanitas* painting: a tall vase of purple columbines

and red hollyhocks encircled by phallic green cucumbers and marrow, a basket of yellow and orange mushrooms, a cut watermelon and leafy branches with crimson-tinged green apples and blackberries — all of this from the forest or the dacha's garden. I stand on a chair and photograph it from above.

Perfect little red apples, China apples, sit on my bedroom shelf.

LETTER FROM ST PETERSBURG

I love Tamara's apartment. It's in the historic centre, just off Nevsky Prospekt. Her building is the soul of baroque, with caryatids of Atlas at intervals along its recessed front stooping and groaning under the weight of the upper storeys. The handsome marble foyer, its curved staircase banistered with iron tendrils, is now pitted with holes, swathed in gloom. The once majestic rooms were long ago partitioned into one- and two-room apartments.

Inside her book-lined room, tall windows look across to the elaborate facades of food and fashion shops. Tamara eats, sleeps, works and entertains in this room. In spite of the clutter, it's charming. Everything in it leads a double life. The tatty couch, with its linen-storage base, converts to her bed. The armchair folds out to become a single bed for guests. The table under the windows is, by turns, desk, dressing table and — with tablecloth — dining table. In one corner a battered grand piano supports stacks of books and papers, a television set, a large vase of flowers, a make-up mirror, cosmetics and an oriental bazaar of personal mementos. Drawings and paintings are squeezed between ceiling-high bookshelves. Above the piano is a portrait of Tamara, with her classical bone structure, chiselled mouth and tragic Akhmatova eyes.

Tamara is just like her apartment — scholarly, cosmopolitan and feminine. And contained. At first her haughty air is intimidating, so her generosity and almost embarrassing thoughtfulness come as a surprise. A few days ago she and I spent hours walking around the vast Peterhof Palace. At the station on the way back she ran off momentarily and reappeared with some bandaids, which she applied to the blistered back of my heel after we sat in the train. She said I'd been limping; I'd hardly noticed.

Tamara is one of the senior curators of art at the Russian Museum — an enviable job, working with such a great collection. Yet her salary is less than a street-sweeper's, just enough to pay her minimal rent and buy food and books, which are (or were) very cheap in Russia. At first it surprised me when she angrily told me how low her salary was — Ada hadn't mentioned hers, and of the two friends, Ada is far more forthcoming. Tamara is very reserved. But now that I know them both a little better I see that Tamara is more political: issues like salary and living conditions are for public discussion, private matters are generally kept to oneself. Ada is the opposite.

The apartment represents freedom to Tamara. Up until a

few years ago she lived in one room with her elderly parents and her son, who is now twenty-seven. He still lives with her, in a windowless space behind a flimsy partition they have erected across the room. His willowy girlfriend is there more often than not. Tamara wishes he would get married and go, but his low income makes this unlikely. She dreams of privacy.

Today Tamara is giving a tea party to introduce me to two of her colleagues. Like all Russians she loves sweets so we walk to Yeliseevsky, an art nouveau cavern of a food shop with a vast chandeliered interior that has changed little since the days of the Tsars. It remained intact through Soviet times because it was patronised by Party officials who could afford to buy its quality vodka and wines, its black or rich red caviar, its varieties of cheeses, German beers and sausages and other luxury imported goods.

Tamara and I buy cheese, bread, chocolates and a large round tin containing her favourite cake — ginger with fig jam. Food is happiness. For years, Tamara tells me, she stood in long queues to buy something that 'wasn't fish'.

As we walk back, wending our way through the crowds of broad Nevsky Prospekt and turning left into her street, she laughingly quotes something she heard on television last night. (Tamara is an insomniac; she reads or watches TV until three or four in the morning.) American and Russian teenagers were talking to each other via a cable link-up. Inevitably, the Americans were curious about Russian attitudes to sex. 'Oh, you know, we are very warm people,' the Russian girl had replied. 'We like sex very much. But the way we live, it's impossible. We don't have a sex life.' Tamara is very taken with the boldness of this girl. 'We don't have a sex life. It's true. It's true,' she repeats. I think it's a consolation to her that a nubile girl has come right out and said it on television.

Inside, Tamara clears the table of books and papers, adding them to the already teetering stacks on the piano.

'Did you study music?' I ask her, curious as to why she keeps a piano that takes up a quarter of the room.

'Yes. I was pianist as young woman, before I study art history.'

'Do you still play?'

'No.' Something in her tone tells me this is the end of that conversation.

We move the table so that two of the guests can sit on the sofa bed. She produces a floral tablecloth from a bulging cupboard, disappears along the corridor and returns with a tray of tea things, and we lay out the food on the table.

Tamara's colleagues Yelena and Eugenia arrive with an older woman, Matilda, an English teacher. She tells me she's delighted at this opportunity to converse with a native English speaker. We crowd around the table, exchanging greetings as Tamara pours the tea. Matilda, grey hair in a French knot and an imitation cameo at the throat of her mauve blouse, proudly tells me she has coached all three women in English, and Ada as well. 'In Soviet times it was necessary for art scholars to be conversant only in Russian, and perhaps some German,' she explains. 'But now they read more widely, and travel to many countries as well, so it is important to be fluent in English. Some, like Yelena,' she nods like a mother hen at Yelena, 'study German and French as well.' I recall that Ada, too, is currently studying German.

I chat with Yelena, who exudes friendliness and curiosity about Australia. With her gleaming pageboy hair and limpid brown eyes, she shines with youth, health and devotion to sculpture. It seems her life revolves around her elderly parents and the Russian Museum, yet she is open, girlish, enthusiastic. She strikes me as highly intelligent, gifted perhaps, for she is unusually young to be the museum's curator of sculpture.

Eugenia is older and more reserved; it seems fitting that her specialty is Russian icons. Even her height and plaited chignon are majestic. She, too, lives with her parents.

With lives undistracted by husbands, children and consumer pursuits, I think to myself, these women *are* their jobs. I feel at home in this room with them, in this cloistered world of female scholarship, me with my fantasy of living high in a tower with servals and ocelots, surrounded by books, paintings and mysterious charts. It occurs to me I'm probably romanticising their lives, so I ask Eugenia, 'At home, do you care for your parents or do they care for you?'

'My mother cares for all of us,' she replies. 'But now she is not so well, it is necessary for me to shop for the food.'

'Is your father in good health?' I ask.

'Yes, he is quite strong, thank you.'

Tamara is setting up a slide-viewing machine she's brought from the museum. Australia is so exotic to Russians — a sunny land at the other edge of the world, a mystery, so Tamara asked me bring some slides of Australian art to show them.

'Do you have interest in the Russian sculpture?' Yelena asks me as I open my boxes of slides.

'All that dark monumental Socialist Realist stuff glorifying the Soviet?' I say, pretending to shudder. 'Yes of course. It's so creepy.'

'Ooh,' she actually claps her hands in delight. 'I would love to show you. You must come to museum tomorrow and I will take you down in big storeroom.'

We arrange the time and place, looking across the table at Tamara, who's growing increasingly agitated. Something in the viewing device refuses to click into place. She passes it around the table and we all have a go but it's unfixable. Cries of disappointment echo around the table.

I've brought a couple of books with me as well and they save the day. The women are particularly taken with the Aboriginal painter, Ginger Riley. He fascinates them: his black skin; his cowboy outfit; his radiant, symbolic paintings with the bird Njuk Njuk, the guardian spirit of the land. Tamara's intrigued, leafing through and through his catalogue, silently shaking her head. Suddenly she stands up, raising her hand for silence. We all obey. She fetches a book from the shelf behind her, finds the page she wants and places it open, next to the Ginger Riley catalogue. Here are figurative works by Kasimir

Malevich — known in the west as the greatest figure of the Russian avant-garde, a pioneer of abstract painting. And it is indeed remarkable that the palettes of these two painters — separated by generations, continents, entirely different cultures and ways of seeing — are uncannily similar. There's something in the spirit, the airiness of the space, that unites the two artists.

The women are very excited — here's an opportunity for an art historical detective game. Has Ginger Riley seen works by Malevich? I don't know. It's possible — he visited Paris. I'm thinking of how we're now so obsessed with cultural and racial differences, we've lost sight of the fact that human beings, throughout history and across continents, have far more in common than is generally acknowledged.

While the women gossip about work I look through a sumptuous book on Russian icons. I've recently been with Ada and Mitri to Novgorod, an icon stronghold, where we did little else but look at the real things. The narrative world of Russian icons, darkly sombre or exquisitely jewel-like, is peopled with angels, martyrs, prophets, protectors and saints performing various miracles. And, with rare exceptions, all these Russian Orthodox movers and shakers, mediators of divine protection, objects of reverence, are male. So are the witnesses, the onlookers, the crowds. All males. It gets to you after a while. I'm curious to see what the assembled company of women feels about this. During a lull in the conversation, I blurt out, 'All these images are of male saints. Why aren't there any women?'

The women look dismayed. Icons are to be revered, not questioned.

'But … the Virgin Mary,' respond Eugenia and Tamara, almost in unison.

'Yes,' I agree. 'There are many Virgin Marys.' Almost as many as there are Christs. 'But you have female saints in Russia. Why are they so rarely depicted in icons?'

'These are mostly stories from the Bible,' Eugenia reminds me.

'The Bible is full of stories about women,' I remind her.

Their puzzled looks tell me they doubt the truth of this.

'Think of Italian art. The Renaissance, the baroque,' I press. 'All those vibrant, beautiful women.'

'But this is the secular art,' responds Eugenia. 'Many of these figures, these women, they take it from the classical mythology, no?'

She has a point there.

'Yes, but not always. There are also religious figures like Suzannah and the Magdelene. The Italians always found a way to put women in their art. There's a joy in the feminine. Even in paintings that focus on men, there's often a woman in the picture. Even if her role is largely decorative.'

Eugenia and Tamara exchange glances.

'The icons are not the decoration,' murmurs Eugenia gravely.

I'd hoped for debate, but it isn't their style. I can see the conversation is upsetting to them. In Russia, a guest's wellbeing is the supreme consideration. If a guest is unhappy, or querulous as I was just now, then the host feels somehow at fault. This is particularly true of Tamara, who goes out of her way to be gracious to me. Besides, my implication that Italian art is in some way superior to Russian art is insulting.

'I'm sorry,' I apologise. 'It's just that women in the west, well, you know, we've learnt to think along certain lines.'

I assure them that the icons are very beautiful, as many of them are, and flick though the book, pointing out my favourites. This soothes them.

I don't tell them what I really think, that it's time for some basic feminist critiques of historical works of art in Russia. They wouldn't understand. Feminism to Tamara, the most intelligent of women, is something a few ratbags in Moscow get up to.

Thoughts I've been having for days come to a head. I can't tell them I despair because these highly educated women, trained analytical thinkers, don't think to ask the simple question, Why? Why are most of the people in these pictures men? This absence of an interrogative spirit seems to me to befog their whole lives. Why are most of the curators in Russian museums women? Why are they paid a pittance for this highly specialised work, requiring years of devoted study? Why are the majority of women not promoted through the system as men are? Why do women, even educated ones like Ada, do all the domestic chores? Why does it fall to women like Yelena and Eugenia to live with and care for their elderly parents? It seems to me that these questions are vitally connected and the answer to them all is obvious. Russia is a country which represses women. Equal education under the Soviet regime has done little to change it. Tamara won't have that. 'Russia is a country which represses *humanity*,' she insists.

Yet I understand. The obsession with icons. The unquestioning reverence for Russia's pre-Soviet history. Recovering from seven decades of totalitarian warfare against their cultural heritage, Russians are busy reclaiming their past. What's left of it. As part of Stalin's program to eradicate religion most of the icons, some as ancient as the tenth century, were burnt, smashed, stolen or sold on the black market to western collectors for peanuts. No wonder the remaining ones are regarded with such reverence. They are the most potent symbol of a past that has become sacred because so much has been lost. Some of Stalin's bullyboys took a particular delight in blowing up those glorious churches, supreme examples of mystical architecture. Very, very few are left of the ancient wooden ones, with their wonderful minarets — exquisite examples of folk art.

And I understand Russian women's distaste for feminism, the unwillingness to take a position, to see themselves as separate from their male fellows. Intelligent Russians loathe ideologies, having had one rammed down their throats for nearly a century.

Heroic, positive and glorifying Russia. The Party mandate for art rings in my head as Yelena leads me through the twentieth century sculpture storerooms of the Russian Museum. Yelena seems particularly fresh in this cheerless environment, schoolgirlish in her crisp white blouse with pleated skirt and maroon cardigan, smooth nut-brown hair shinier than ever. We pass shelf after shelf, unit after unit, of grim bronze heads. Moustached Party officials, stern generals, bony factory workers, wholesome farm workers, the occasional artist, art critic or theatre manager — the ones who toed the line. (Most did.) And Lenin — angry, exhorting, gesticulating, grimacing. Lenin of the thunderous brow.

'Where's Stalin?' I ask, surprised that the craggy face hasn't yet presented itself.

'Oh,' laughs Yelena, 'The statues of Stalin they are so, so big. The artists, you know they always felt obliged to make him very huge. We cannot fit them into our storerooms. They must remain outside.'

She leads me down broad stone steps to a cavernous room which houses an army of towering figures. Soldiers and farm workers. Generals and factory workers. Sailors and aviators. Lenin and more Lenin. Larger than life figure groups: clusters of Party dignitaries (here is Stalin, a central figure in his general's uniform), the war-wounded being tended, the glorious dead. Standing victoriously astride, banner aloft, is a manful child posturing nobly.

'This small boy was big Soviet hero,' says Yelena. 'When

he was nine years old he denounced his parents to Soviet authorities and they were sent to labour camp. He was seen as desirable example of the unselfish devotion to Party. This sculpture of him was made to act as the inspiration to Soviet youth.'

'Do you think it did?' I ask, wondering if the little horror ever regretted it.

'This is a big question we cannot yet answer. Stalin had strong faith in art as the propaganda. But he get this idea from Trotksy and Stalin, he doesn't really understand the art enough to judge the impact. Maybe the Socialist Realist art doesn't so much persuade the people as Stalin believe.'

'Do you mean that people aren't as stupid as he thought they were?'

'Yes.'

There's the marquet, itself enormous, of my favourite Soviet sculpture: the dynamic young hero and heroine marching forward against the wind, their hair streaming behind them in horizontal ripples, he triumphantly brandishing a hammer, she a sickle. So seductively art deco. They so sweep you up in the kinesis of progress, you don't even notice their mindlessness.

'Let's stand still for a minute,' I say to Yelena when we reach the middle of the room. I want to look around at these silent figures, frozen forever in their heroic postures. This is a graveyard of Socialist Realist sculpture, of Stalinism. I want to feel spooked.

It works. In the silence and stillness the three-dimensional figures, many of them life-size, become strangely potent. A layer of dust covers everything, sealing it in time past. Mysterious forms lurk beneath draped white sheets. The room takes on a prescience, becoming haunted. So Stalin destroyed thousands of artists to achieve — what? — ossified effigies of Soviet Man. As I glance over these countless ghosts I notice we're not the only passers-by. There's Peter the Great, with his fleshy, sensuous, handsome face. That great collector and connoisseur, that lover of extravagant beauty, builder of sumptuous palaces, founder of a magical city, rivalrous wooer of Europe's best, how he must despise being in such drab company. Still, he has one thing to be thankful for. The Soviets never took him on. Too awesome for them. Lenin shifted the capital of Russia back to Moscow, steering clear of St Petersburg. So while Moscow's architectural heritage was systematically destroyed, making way for the progressive Stalinist style, the centre of St Petersburg remained miraculously intact. Still Peter's city, the Venice of the North.

Something else lurks in this storeroom. Paradoxically, it's the most disturbing thing here, yet it is the one thing that isn't a ghost. It's very much alive, highly expressive, devilishly amusing. A riotous company of theatrical figures, giant rag dolls — they would terrify a small child — seems to be making its way slowly, inexorably, across the room. These dancing, grinning agents of misrule — one is aloft a ladder held by two others — are flour white. Ghoulish. One poses as an impresario in top hat and tails, another as a sparkling ballerina, the fat one — triple chinned, mouth wide open — as an opera singer, the monocled one a theatre critic. Somehow you know that these characters are only playing at being what they're dressed as — they are really up to something else, something chaotic. They resemble nothing but themselves, yet you can see they have their origins in St Petersburg's desperate Dada theatricality of the twenties, the last carnival before the dying of the light. They're quintessentially Russian, and they're the gleeful spirit of anarchy itself. They remind me a little of Anatole. Dangerous and untrustworthy as they are, in this mausoleum they're a breath of fresh air.

'When were these made?' I ask Yelena.

'In early 1980s.'

'So recent?' Thank god, I think. Irreverence, fearlessness, devil-take-it. At last.

'St Petersburg art before Stalin love to make the reference to the theatre,' says Yelena. 'It is so interesting that recent art make this connection too, no?'

'Very,' I agree.

'I have a nightmare,' she confides.

'What is it?' I ask.

'That I am locked in this storeroom. All night.'

I've had enough of Socialist Realist sculpture; my mind and senses are numbed by it. It's time to get out into the fresh air, take a walk in the Summer Garden, look up at the lacy canopy of lime trees, the ethereal faces of classical statues.

As Yelena and I walk back through the storerooms I keep my eyes to the ground, and that's why I see a clay portrait sculpture tucked away in the corner of a bottom shelf. Now I've spotted it, I can't imagine how I missed it on the way in, for it has such presence it almost leaps off the shelf.

We pause and Yelena places it on a higher shelf so I can stare it full in the face. It's the head of a tough old woman. Sounds dull, doesn't it? But this old woman is fierce, totemic, a cross between Gloria Swanson and an Aztec emperor. You can tell she was once a beauty — high cheekbones, great hooded eyes, full lips that age has dragged down at the corners. She reminds me of those eccentric, overpainted old women you used to see around Sydney and Melbourne, the ones with too much rouge on their cheeks. Women of the twenties they were. So is she, and like them she wears a lot of white face powder. Her mouth's painted bright paprika, matching her earrings and the neck of her dress. Her right eye is rimmed with kohl, confident; her left looks sightless, fearful. This portrait is everything that Stalin devoted so much institutionalised hatred to eradicating — she is modernist, primitive, expressive and defiantly strange.

'Who made this?' I ask Yelena.

'Ah, you like it very much,' she says, beaming. 'I am so pleased because it is special for me also. Artist is Pelageya Shuriga and this is portrait bust of her friend Parfatskaya, who was textile artist. I think you would be most interested in story of Shuriga's life. Recently we had Shuriga retrospective at this museum and,' she continues proudly, 'I help work on this exhibition. We produce catalogue with version in English too and I would like to present you with copy of this.'

'I'd love a copy. Thanks, Yelena. Do you have time to tell me about her life or are you busy?'

'Yes, I must tell you. It is very important people from other countries know about the excellent Russian artists who are not so famous. Even in Russia we didn't know about Shuriga. Like other artists who dare to work in modern style, all her life she was invisible. She was old woman when she died in 1980 but she has attained her exhibition only recently, many years after her death.'

We go up one of the narrow flights of wooden stairs behind the museum's exhibition spaces, originally the rooms of the Mikhail Palace. When we reach the top, Yelena indicates for me to sit in the broad space with its muted light and dark timber floors, rather like a large attic room. She goes into her office where she works with two or three other curators and returns, handing me the attractive colour catalogue of Shuriga, the sculptor who publicly toed the Party line but who, when she could, secretly made the works she was born to make, ones with titles like *Queen of the Jungle*. Her portrait of Parfatskaya is on the cover of the catalogue and I notice it's consciously defiant, for she's streaked the white face with blue and ochre patterns. War paint.

'When was Shuriga born?' I ask.

'In 1900, very symbolic,' says Yelena. 'This is beginning of great flourishing of modernism in Russia and Shuriga grow up with this. You know Russia, and particularly St Petersburg, was among world leaders of avant-garde at this time.'

'Yes,' I say. 'And at first the Bolsheviks approved of this, didn't they? A revolutionary art for a revolutionary people?'

'Yes, this is true. But is more Trotsky's idea, who is sensitive to the art. Lenin hated the modernism and particularly Stalin too because he is military man and very conservative. Stalin want realistic art that everybody can understand so he can use it for the propaganda. And art academicians are very powerful in Russia at this time and they advise Stalin that heroic styles of nineteenth century are more powerful to invent inspiring message of heroic Soviet people. So in 1920s he outlaw formalism. All artists must work in style of Socialist Realism. Ones who don't are sent to Kazakhstan.'

'What's Kazakhstan?'

'Labour camp, far way. People who are sent there do not return. Of course the artists who do not obey have many various fates. We can't know how many thousands are tormented or murdered or put in psychiatric hospitals or other such terrible things, but we say "sent to Kazakhstan" as general expression meaning Stalin kick them out of the way.

'Of course this law about the Socialist Realism make life very difficult for Shuriga because, you know,' Yelena laughs in her bubbly way, 'she had irrepressible temperament. She loves the radiant colour, like Kandinsky. But Kandinsky goes to live in Europe and has the freedom — he is very famous in the west, no?

'Very,' I say. 'One of the greats of modernism. I was taught that two of the three pioneers of pure abstraction were Russians — Kandinsky and Malevich.'

'Yes? I am so pleased for Malevich because Stalin persecute him terribly. Malevich try to reconstruct himself as figurative painter in 1920s and he succeed but really, many people believe this is what kill him, to exist against his spirit like this. He was such great theoretician about the abstract art and after his death his family are very afraid, and they burn his precious writings. Ah, we have lost so much,' she says, shaking her head sorrowfully.

'But we must talk about Shuriga,' she remembers, recovering her smile. 'What is so interesting is Shuriga never travel, but she has such fascination with exotic countries, she have instinct for art of these countries as if she has been there. You can hardly believe this. I show you.' Yelena flicks through the catalogue. 'Look at this,' she says, pointing to a colour photograph of a large sculpture. Shuriga has really let rip with this one. It's a startlingly barbaric figure — a fertility goddess with pregnant belly and enormous breasts, bejewelled and tattooed like a primitive warlord.

'She sculpt this when she is seventy-one years old, when state control is becoming not so strict,' says Yelena. 'She call it *Mexico*. It has atmosphere of this country, no?

'Yes, the folk art. It's like some Amazon queen,' I say. 'She must have seen something that inspired it.'

Yelena shrugs. 'Maybe old photograph. But, you know, is very much Shuriga personality.'

'Maybe it was her private goddess,' I say.

Yelena laughs and claps her hands. 'Yes, this could be true.'

How unimaginably difficult it must have been for Shuriga to dance to Stalin's tune. It's inevitable that long periods of her creative life were wasted, as Yelena now tells me they were. 'In her twenties she worked at Leningrad porcelain factory, purely as a technician.'

'Was this another way the state controlled artists?' I ask her. 'Turned them into workers?'

'Of course. But when she is thirty-five Shuriga is placed in charge of factory's museum. This is interesting for her because is very good collection that includes Suprematist ceramics of Kasimir Malevich. But most important, here at last she can make little studio for herself, behind curtain in storeroom. She model heads and figures of factory's porcelain artists, and the cleaners and guards. She follow Socialist Realist formula,' Yelena shakes her head, smiling with affection at an image of a female factory worker, 'but Shuriga is sly you know, very clever, or maybe can't stop herself, because she give these figures the modernist energy.'

I see what Yelena is smiling at. The female factory worker, all straight and correct, wears an apron like the wildest Kandinsky.

'And look at this one. Such psychological depth,' enthuses Yelena. Violence and stupidity lurk beneath the expressively modelled features of an impassive male guard. 'And Shuriga is very amusing, witty woman as well,' Yelena continues.

'Maybe you notice in museum that mother and child is favourite subject in Russian art. Before Revolution and in Soviet times too.' She looks at me inquiringly.

'Yes. I wondered about those Soviet ones of farm workers smiling at their babies,' I say. 'Sometimes the women are like Madonnas. Do you think some Soviet artists chose this subject because it was a hidden way of painting religious pictures?'

Yelena is already shaking her head. 'No, no. Some people have this theory but it is not correct.'

'I didn't know about the theory,' I say, certain that this is how many Soviet artists sublimated their religious instincts. 'It's just that some of them have that Madonna and child radiance to them.'

'No. This is love for the colour,' she frowns, making me curious as to why she doesn't like this idea. Perhaps it's a currently fashionable debate in Russia — like the one about Malevich's suprematism being influenced by icons — and she's bored with it.

'May we return to Shuriga?' she asks politely, reminding me for a moment of Ada's and Tamara's stubbornness with ideas, which they are far less polite about. I nod. 'I tell you just before Shuriga is witty. Look at this one how she make joke about mother and child always so smiling and harmonious, and here she show real life is not like this.' The beautifully modelled little sculpture is an unsentimental slice of domestic life — the mother, arm raised, spanking the child she holds across her lap.

'Art must be slap in the face of public taste,' laughs Yelena. 'Russian futurists say this in 1912 manifesto. You knew this?'

'No, but I love it.'

'Shuriga's fertile period of creativity is halted by Second World War,' continues Yelena. 'Shuriga and museum's treasures are evacuated to Ural district, very isolated place. For duration of war she lives in barracks among sealed crates. She has not even materials to make the sculptures.' Yelena leans forward, eyes shining in admiration of her heroine. 'But Shuriga can no longer be prevented. She make the huge drawings.'

I look. No wonder Yelena's excited. The drawings are monumental, primitive female nudes with curiously schematised, unerotic, unmaternal breasts. They're confronting, cerebral figures, women of the creative intellect, not, for all their nakedness, women of the body.

'Shuriga is very nervous about these and for the rest of her life keeps them hidden in her apartment. After war she doesn't know what to do. Her artistic creation … shrivelled up. For twenty years she makes few amusing pieces of no importance. But then,' Yelena's voice rises with enthusiasm, 'when Shuriga is in her sixties, her creative strength return and she produces disarming body of strong paintings about cats.'

I see that Shuriga's cats are like no other's. Not tamed, domestic pussykins, but physically powerful, covert creatures, fierce guardians of their intellectual independence with titles like *Feline Philosopher*.

'Do you think they're disguised self-portraits?' I ask Yelena.

'I think this myself. I am in complete agreement with you,' she enthuses, with her delighted little clap. 'They are her psychological strength and the philosophical forbearance.'

'Your English is very good, Yelena,' I smile, tickled by the quaint precision of the sentence.

'Do you think so, really?' she asks, the good student again.

'Yes, really. So, finally, near the end of her life, the relaxation of Party dictates allows Shuriga some freedom of spirit to sculpt her monumental Amazons?'

'Yes, and astonishing works like portrait of Parfatskaya. She waits all her life, until she is seventy. It's so terrible. If it were not for her daughter, who kept works and brought them to attention of Russian Museum, she would be evaporated. It takes sixteen years after her death for us to have privilege of acquaintance with such important artist.'

———•◦•———

I make it to the Summer Garden at last. I have an hour to myself, an hour of delicious privacy, before I have to meet Ada. I find the most secluded spot, a wooden seat in a shadowy linden grove near Peter the Great's modest wooden summer house, and take deep breaths of solitude. My life's been crowded with visits and outings and people for nearly three weeks now and I'm used to having weekends at least to myself. Here, by the time I arrive back at what is for the moment home, I'm so tired after my full days that I usually boil some eggs or eat fruit and cheese and fall asleep after ten minutes reading in bed. My head feels crammed with new information. And it's not going to leave me in peace now.

I think of Shuriga's monumental drawings of women. For their time, they were extraordinary. They still are. In a normal artistic life cycle, one unshackled by state dictates, she would have developed and perfected this theme of the monumental asexual eternal feminine and, no doubt, have provided inspiration to countless women, and perhaps men, artists. She transformed, completely toppled, the way woman is traditionally portrayed in art. I think of how her obsession with the eternal feminine became sublimated into a ten-year preoccupation with the eternal feline, and smile to myself. It seems to have been a clever compromise. What orthodoxy-sniffing Party official would care to make himself ridiculous by interrogating portraits of cats? I suppose it's some compensation that she's been acknowledged as an important artist. But for the times and the country in which she lived, she might have been a great one.

I return to the museum to meet Ada. An exhibition of contemporary Russian art has just gone on display in one of the main galleries and she wants me to look at it with her.

We make for a large painting at the end, attracted like magnets, and stand before it.

'This is not like a painting by a woman,' announces Ada.

'No? Why not?' I ask.

'It is too … strong for a woman.'

What can I say? To me, an Australian schooled in traditions of liberal democracy, feminism, postmodernism and what have you, it is very much like a painting by a woman. To Ada, an outstanding curator and art historian schooled in Russian traditions of scholarship, it is not. Even our responses to historical artworks like Shuriga's are worlds apart. I see them as radical works of a feminine consciousness of the world. Ada, and even Yelena who must be ten years her junior, see them as the idiosyncratic works of an 'irrepressible temperament'. Anyway, Shuriga is history — another country — and we are now looking at a St Petersburg work painted in 1997.

Looking at this large, striking self-portrait by a young woman artist, I guess that it's not its strength that leads Ada to consider it unwomanly, not entirely. The artist looks very Russian. She has painted herself full figure, wearing a long skirt, boots and a jacket. She stands against a simple painterly backdrop. The painting is entirely without adornment. There is no clue, no symbol, no incipient narrative to give any hints about her life or her interests. You don't need them. Here she is, in the full force of her presence, staring out calmly at the viewer, just the glint of a challenge in her eye. This is the portrait of a woman whose life is taken up with painting, and little else. It embodies two qualities that have been impossible to attain for the generations of my dear friends at the Russian Museum. Their lives are too difficult, too exhausting, too crowded with other people and their needs. This young artist has embraced solitude, had learnt to stand alone. And she is supremely, unshakably self-confident. Her painting lingers in my thoughts. I like to think of it as a symbol of the new generation of Russian women.

MAN WITH A VIDEO CAMERA

Anatole and Irina compulsively document their life on video. Each day is transformed into a theatrical extravaganza with neighbours and friends drawn in to play themselves, invented characters, extras in crowd scenes. How effortlessly they combine their Russian qualities — innate theatricality and deep sense of community — with their intoxication with the west: their capitalist aspirations and love of consumer goods. And how effortlessly Anatole combines buffoonery with a Machiavellian intelligence. I sometimes wonder if he is aware as he films his days that he is documenting the rise of the new Russian middle-class.

Tonight Ada and I are throwing a dinner party. Irina has created a performance we'll all participate in afterwards, which, inevitably, Anatole will video.

Mitri has gone to Moscow on business so Ada is staying with me.

The electricity is faulty and the lights blink on and off or cut out for hours. Luckily the stove runs on gas cylinders. We've been without hot water for ten days. To wash our bodies, clothes, hair, we pour pots of water heated on the stove into Ada's makeshift washstand: a red plastic bucket that sits on a wobbly stool in the bath.

I'm becoming accustomed to the precariousness of domestic life here; it can be almost fun, a bit like camping. I, too, am learning to make do, so when Felix the kitten springs up on the curtains and pulls the entire arrangement down on top of himself, I fold the curtains away temporarily, and seize the opportunity to utilise the curtain rod as a clothes line.

In preparation for the dinner party, today is to be an unusually domestic one for me, devoted to cleaning, shopping and cooking.

I've discovered Kuznechny, a wonderful food market that dates back to pre-Revolutionary times. It's St Petersburg's best.

On this drizzly afternoon I squeeze onto a decrepit, jam-packed trolleybus, leaving the grim twentieth century behind for the picturesquely grotty, Dostoevskian world of Vladimirskaya. I cross its busy square, littered with construction equipment and the rubble of deferred public works, and walk past old women clustered outside onion-domed Vladimir Church selling bunches of home-grown red and orange asters. Just down the road is the modest but comfortable apartment with the large, green-felt-topped desk where Dostoevski wrote *The Brothers Karamazov*.

I walk through the Greek temple entrance to the market,

go to the marvellous cheese stall just inside and buy my favourite fresh curd cheese. The two smiling women behind the counter remember I'm a foreigner and offer me samples they slice from butter-coloured rounds of cheese. One tastes like a parmesan, another a provolone. I buy them and the women press on me two other types as gifts so I blow them a kiss as I leave. They love this, smiling and waving as if they're seeing me off on a voyage.

I walk past white-tiled islands of produce, attracted by the amazing sight of enormous golden honeycombs still thick with buzzing bees. That's what I love about this market, its

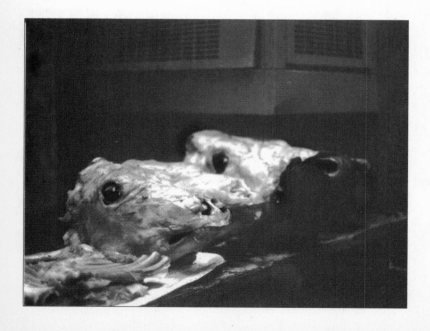

earthiness, and its surreal blend of the beautiful and the shocking. I pass platters of amber-coloured caviar, artfully stacked trays of pure red pomegranates and thick green clusters of grapes hanging high above tiers of watermelons. Behind here, meat stalls display the macabre evidence of exactly what it is so many of us eat: neat rows of lambs' heads, the flesh cut from them so that only bloody red bone with staring eyes remains; gutted rabbit corpses splayed in the missionary position, their legs still wearing furry white socks, front paws placed together in prayer.

The meat here looks trustworthy. Still, I won't be buying any. A few months ago mad cow disease broke out in England, destroying their export market, and news is that the meat was secretly sold to Russia. I buy two chicken corpses instead, their heads still intact, dead eyes filmed white.

———•◦•———

Ada's finishing work an hour early today. We meet up at four near the statue of Pushkin outside the Russian Museum, and walk to Nevsky Prospekt past the majestic Hotel Europa with its corbel figures of muscular Atlases, a sight that never fails to make me feel excited to be in St Petersburg.

Rounding the corner we pass a wizened old woman crouched in a kneeling position who taps her black-shawled head repeatedly, dementedly, against the footpath. In front of her is a piece of ragged fabric on which a few coins have been thrown.

I let Ada walk ahead and, finding a 1000 ruble note, quickly place it on the rag, but Ada turns her head and catches me.

'I told you, you must not to do this,' she says angrily.

I shrug. 'It's only a thous—'

'Why must you give money to mafia?' she demands.

'You don't really know that, Ada. It's just something people say.'

'This woman work for mafia. I am telling you.'

'What if she doesn't? She's been here all day, doubled up like that. She's here every day. She deserves to be paid.'

'You do not understand. Begging in Russia is business.'

'So?'

'So beggar doesn't keep the money.'

Ada and I never agree on this issue.

We board a bus headed homewards and alight at an outdoor supermarket on a unsightly, dusty, half dug-up stretch of road. The supermarket is an assortment of fifty or so specialty stalls, like kiosks, at the entrance to Lesnaya metro. We buy wine, vodka and groceries. I hate coming here because it's so ugly, so I buy a bunch of enormous red chrysanthemums to cheer myself up, as well as a packet of Gitanes for an incredible twenty-five cents even though I don't smoke any more. For years Gitanes haven't been available in Australia because their French manufacturers refused to mar the beautifully designed packet and its silhouetted image of a woman with our government health warning. I buy them as a keepsake because I love this blue packet that hasn't changed since the 1930s, because the word Gitanes means gypsies, and because I used to so love smoking them. One puff of that heady tobacco and I was in Paris.

Ada walks to a stall selling toilet rolls and I trail after her. She says a few words to the young woman attendant who leans against the back of the stall with her arms folded, her eyes fixed on some indefinite point beyond our shoulders as she mumbles a sullen reply. Ada shrugs in mild annoyance and turns to walk away.

'Why did she say?' I ask.

'That I cannot buy anything.'

'Why?'

'Because is too late. Shop close at five.'

I check my watch and it's a minute past five.

'But what does it matter? She's just standing there doing nothing.'

Ada shrugs and pulls at my arm. 'Doesn't matter. Let us go.' She's resigned to this lumpenproletariat contempt for humanity that shop and service agency employees in Russia still dish out, a hangover from the Soviet days of queues and bribes. It's an aspect of life here I find intolerable.

I look at the girl. She's staring at the button on my coat and slowly raises her eyes to look into mine with icy contempt. I feel in my pocket, find a few 500 ruble coins, slam them on the counter and, leaning across, take a couple of toilet rolls. I put them in Ada's shopping bag and we walk off. The girl doesn't move.

———•◦•———

As Ada turns the key in the lock of the second steel door we hear the third one being unlocked from the inside and the deep tones of an excited greeting. Mitri has arrived back early from Moscow. We're treated to beer and bear hugs.

Leaving Mitri and Ada to catch up in the kitchen I walk into the main room, the bedroom-cum-living room, and to my embarrassment discover that an army of elves has tidied it. The curtains have been replaced on the windows and four chairs have been placed in the room, my clothes, now dry, draped neatly over their backs.

Mitri assures me it was like this when he arrived.

———•◦•———

In the small kitchen Ada and I roll up our sleeves and prepare our banquet. Ada makes separate cucumber, mushroom and potato salads with her delicious sour-cream dressing, and a rich borscht with pork, sage and dill-pickled cucumbers. I wrestle with lemon chicken, my repertoire limited because the oven doesn't work.

The subtle aroma of diced flesh is too much for Felix the kitten. He stands on his hind legs like a dog, begging politely, then sits back on his haunches, paws aloft, comfortably holding the pose for minutes at a time between the tidbits we throw him.

This is the least of Felix's accomplishments. Kitty litter is unheard of in Russia and, incredibly, Ada has trained him to use the toilet; he sits perched at the front of the toilet seat, a tiny black and white mite with lifted tail and the sharpest intelligent little face, and always aims perfectly. He reminds me of Behemoth, the cat in Bulgakov's novel *The Master and Margarita*, who performs feats like hanging off the handrail of a moving tram with one paw as he stands on the running board, holding aloft in the other paw a glass of wine, toasting pedestrians.

'Felix the cat, the wonderful, wonderful cat,' sing Ada and I.

Mitri's beaming Slavic face appears around the door, asking when we'll be finished with our chopping and giggling; he's in the process of transforming the bedsit into a dining room and he needs to move the table in there.

The phone rings and Ada goes into the hall to answer it. She listens patiently to the caller, interjecting, her voice becoming progressively louder until she's shouting. Do I detect humour? Then Mitri joins in, shouting, laughing. They both shout together and Ada bangs the receiver down.

She returns to the kitchen.

'What's going on?' I ask.

'Anatole tell me that Mitri must make the line for the clothes so that you do not destroy the apartment,' she says.

'What!' I say, outraged. 'Did you tell him it was Felix who pulled the curtains down?'

'Yes, of course, but he choose not to believe.'

'This is embarrassing,' I say.

'No, you must not be. Anatole like to make the joke. He is troublemaker.' I've just taught her this word and she welcomes the opportunity to use it. 'Mitri say that Anatole must fix the electricity, then maybe Mitri will fix the line. Then Anatole say we are putting on dramatic performance tonight in his apartment and we must pay. And Mitri say Anatole makes the film of this performance so he must pay us.'

Mitri roars with laughter and Ada, serious now, shouts at him, 'And you must to make the line for the clothes.'

———•◦•———

Noisy greetings announce the arrival of Anatole and Irina who've driven into the centre and collected Tamara as well.

Anatole comes into the kitchen, moustache bristling and wicked eyes beaming with pleasure — over the clothesline incident I suppose. I let him have it. 'How dare you come into my room and rearrange my washing?' I snarl. 'The next time you feel like letting yourself in ...'

Words tumble out of my mouth and of course Anatole can understand none of them, but he wags his head in contrition and sorrowfully looks at the floor nevertheless. Suddenly, inspired, he points his index finger in the air, points at the video camera he's carrying, turns it on, points it at me and makes a winding motion for me to continue. I look into the lens and really let him have it. He's delighted. Before he lets me shoo him out of the kitchen he inexplicably films the top of the stove and a close-up of a chicken leg.

Now that Mitri's taken the table there's nothing to dish up the chicken on. I look around the kitchen wondering what to do. I'm unwilling to put the hideous blackened saucepan on the dining table and there are no serving dishes. The only available flat surface is inside the abraded porcelain sink where we wash the dishes. It's another make-do situation. I force toilet paper up the dripping tap so it won't leak onto the food and place a dinner plate in the sink, spoon the chicken onto it and pass it to Ada who carries it in and returns for the next one.

I join them and Mitri tells us about his trip to Moscow. He went there to buy motor oil, which is much cheaper there than in St Petersburg, and he'll resell it here. On the long trip south, in the middle of nowhere, he pulled over on the side of the road to sleep. In the small hours of the morning he was woken up by a young prostitute banging on his window, saying, 'Go with me.'

'Did she have a car?' I ask.

'No.'

'What was she doing in that deserted place on her own? How did she get there?'

He shrugs.

I shiver at the image of the dark, desolate highway and the solitary girl, desperate for money. There are tens of thousands of young Russian women in this situation. 'Poor things,' I say. 'What a terrible way to make a living.'

'I think they like it,' says Tamara disdainfully.

And there you have it. Who could be kinder, more sympathetic than Tamara and Ada? But present them with a beggar, a prostitute, and their generous hearts turn to stone. Is this to do with collective terror at how easy it is to slip beyond the pale in Russia? Or does it have a more sinister ancestry in Soviet brainwashing that insisted on denunciation and hatred of difference?

———•◦•———

I clear the table and prepare dessert so they can speak comfortably in Russian without being concerned for me.

When I return Ada tells me Irina and Anatole are considering selling the apartment.

'But you must not to worry. It will not be for many months yet. Irina has friends who wish to buy apartment but they are afraid. They will buy from Irina because she is friend and it is safe.'

In the first years of perestroika, when property became privatised, many of the few Russians who could afford to purchase apartments didn't do so because they were afraid of the financial risk. Anatole and Irina took that risk and it's obviously paid off.

'What did Anatole pay for this apartment?' I ask.

'Seven thousand American dollars. This was three years ago. Now Anatole want to sell it for twelve thousand.'

'Pretty good profit.'

'Yes. But Irina's friends must save more money and it will take few more months. You met these friends last week at Irina's birthday party, Nadezsha and Alexander, her husband.'

'Nadezsha? I though she was a friend of yours, Ada. Is she the one that works at Pavlovsk Palace?'

'Yes, we are all friends. We go to Pavlovsk next week, so you will see her again. And her husband Alexander is scientist. You remember?'

'Not much.' I only remember his sour face. He seemed old and grumpy. 'But I remember how stylish Nadezsha is. So they really want to buy this apartment? I thought Nadezsha would want to live in the centre or near Pavlovsk.'

'Of course. But they can afford to buy only here.'

'What about Mitri? Will it be difficult for him to rent another apartment?'

'Not so difficult but is better he rent from friend like Anatole.'

As Anatole replenishes our vodka glasses the lights go out and we're pitched into utter blackness. My Russian friends go on eating and talking as if nothing has happened and Anatole even manages to fill my glass. I wonder if they've all learnt to see in the dark.

Over dessert of curd cheese and figs, Irina becomes more animated than usual, words tumbling effusively out of her mouth. This is her moment. Irina loves to act and direct. She's management committee chairwoman of her block of flats and I imagine she performs this and her similar role at the St Petersburg School of Art excellently. She's tied a silk scarf sweatband-style around her blonde curls and its sea blue matches her almond eyes. She has one of those adorable up-turned smiling mouths so she invariably looks like the pussycat who got the cream, but cross Irina and she's a tiger. She's the perfect wife for Anatole.

Tamara listens politely to Irina's instructions; now there are two women who are worlds apart. Anatole, deep in concentration as he rolls his cigarette, is unusually low key. He doesn't seem all that interested in the proceedings.

The lights come back on.

The first scene of the video is to be set in a disco, Ada informs me. While the men move furniture to clear a large space Irina plants a kiss on my cheek and Ada translates her instructions. Mitri and I must dance up close to the wall with our backs to the room. 'You must to dance like crazy completely mad person. You must to make the pattern of the abstract energy, like artistic pattern, but it must be in the motion.'

'Okay,' I say.

Mitri scratches his head and looks down at his pot belly.

Irina and Ada go off to Irina's apartment to change into their costumes.

Anatole sets up a cassette player and adjusts his video camcorder.

Tamara stands in the opposite corner of the room holding a large torch.

Giggling excitedly, the two female leads reappear as sixties disco queens, Ada, her eyes black with mascara, unrecognisable in skimpy gold lamé hot-pants and Courreges-style white boots and sunglasses. Irina features a silver lamé mini and micro-top and narrow peacock-green wraparounds, her hair teased to buggery. Wherever did she get those amazing outfits? They look like the genuine article.

Anatole stands on the couch with camcorder poised. We take up our positions. Lights out. Vintage Blondie blasts from the cassette player and in the flickering light Mitri and I jump around frenetically as instructed, Irina and Ada doing pretty much the same centre stage.

I feel uncomfortable for Tamara, whose job it is to direct the torch at the ceiling and jiggle its switch on and off to simulate flashing discotheque lighting. It's inappropriate for her to be doing something so undignified and I'm a little surprised she's going along with it.

A yell from Irina and it's Cut, not a moment too soon for Mitri.

Irina and Ada stand either side of Anatole to watch the scene on the viewer. As soon as he plays it Anatole cops a volley of outraged Russian from Irina while Ada looks across at me shaking her head mournfully. 'It's terrible,' she says.

We all gather around to look. Anatole replays it, his face expressionless. I'm surprised at how good the effect is, how it really does have the feel of a crowded disco. The problem is that Tamara can clearly be seen flashing the torch in the left of the picture, which of course destroys the illusion. Irina's still screaming at Anatole, who remains expressionless.

We do it again.

Same effect, but even worse. This one shows Anatole's foot, which sends Irina into a frenzy.

'I think Anatole does this on purpose,' Ada whispers to me.

From the rhythms of Irina's tongue-lashing I gather she's delivering Anatole an ultimatum.

She and Ada adjust their clothes, preparing to do the scene a third time. I catch Anatole's eye and with absolute deadpan seriousness he holds up the camera with one hand, points to himself with the other and mouths something I don't catch.

I shrug incomprehension.

Surreptitiously looking around the room, he points to himself and mouths the word again. 'Vertov.'

I head for the sunroom where I can break into giggles without being seen. If Irina saw me laughing in what would appear to be collusion with Anatole, she'd never forgive me.

Anatole's parodying Dziga Vertov, the great Russian pioneer of documentary film-making. Vertov said that the role of cinema was to report the day-to-day reality of life rather than inventing stories with plots and characters. The joke is that Irina is trying to direct a video with invented characters that tells a story, and Anatole is undermining this by filming the reality of the situation — six people in a room making a video.

Vertov's masterpiece, *Man with a Movie Camera*, which he made in 1929, showed a typical day in Moscow, from dawn to dusk. Like life itself the film juxtaposed the banal — shots of a traffic light changing, wheels turning, a woman washing her hair — with the miraculous — the birth of a child. Now I understand Anatole's close-up of the chicken leg.

Vertov's film was acclaimed in America under the title *Russian Life*. Needless to say, Stalin, who had initially approved *Man with a Movie Camera*'s revolutionary celebration of machinery and working life, banned the film on grounds of formalist error in the 1930s and Vertov's output was thereafter severely restricted. Nevertheless he is acclaimed in the west as the father of *cinéma-vérité*.

Sharing Anatole's secret joke is going to make the rest of the evening very difficult for me.

I return to the fold and Anatole allows Take Three to proceed without a hitch, which is just as well because at the end of it Mitri's gasping.

He and Anatole carry the table and chairs back into the room in preparation for the next scene. Irina and Ada go off for a costume change while Tamara and I discuss our trip to Pushkinskaya next week. This was once known as Tsars' Village and has a magnificent group of palaces, Tamara tells me proudly. She generously gives whole mornings or afternoons to showing me the innumerable palaces outside St Petersburg and insists it allows her to catch up with her colleagues who work at them, but she also seems to love the palaces themselves.

'Old Russian name was Tsarskoe Zelo and I think you know this place from Russian literature,' she says.

Indeed I do. We also plan to visit an elderly woman who's promised to arrange for me an introduction to Galina Petrovna Morkovin, a fascinating person, I'm told, whose mother was a member of the old St Petersburg aristocracy. Tamara and I are deep in conversation when we hear Irina return and begin to berate Anatole again. Ada comes into the room shaking her head.

'Anatole makes the film of such crazy stupid things,' Ada whispers to us with a puzzled expression. 'Why is he in bathroom filming bucket on chair in bath? I do not understand this.' She looks at me sharply. 'No, you must not to laugh, Vika. This is not so funny. It is very upsetting for Irina. Sometimes I think he deliberately make the trouble for their marriage. He is big troublemaker.'

The lights go off. The others return to the room and we sit in the dark waiting for the lights to come back on so we can continue videoing. They don't.

Groping in the dark, Tamara locates the torch. Not trusting its batteries, Ada uses it to light her way into the kitchen and fetches a few candles. I find a papier-mâché candelabrum I've bought as a gift for Australian friends, red and gold decoration on a black background in the traditional Russian style. We place it in the centre of the table, put the candles in it and light them. This has a calming effect on all of us. We sit at the table, staring into the candle flames, a little mesmerised by them. Silence. Anatole shoots a close-up of a candle flame. Irina says nothing and I don't dare look at him.

He steps back slowly until we're all in the shot, sitting in a circle around the table, talking in the candlelight. '*Prekrasno!*' he says huskily. '*Mistichesko.*' So beautiful. A mystical circle.

Now he has his miracle.

MUSEUM OF MY DREAMS

———◆◆◆———

Thus a foetus or an angel
opening its milky eyes
sways in a formaldehyde jar
and begs to be returned to the skies
                    Nicolai Zabolotsky, 1913

These lines are more than a metaphor for the mystical effects of St Petersburg's white nights. Their inspiration is a real baby, a 300 year old one who floats at the bottom of a glass cylinder, head hacked from his body and blue eyes fixed beseechingly upwards.

I've put off going to Peter the Great's Museum of Ethnography because it sounds dull. The one photograph I've seen of it, taken in 1937, is even more discouraging; it shows the entire building obliterated by a gigantic banner of Stalin's face; Stalin imprints himself over St Petersburg's founder — the 'popular bully', as Nabokov described Peter, is obliterated by the unpopular one. Nevertheless I've been feeling a sense of duty toward it for over six weeks now — nearly as long as I've been here — so I mention it to my chief advisors. Ada sniffs disdainfully and Tamara screws up her face in disgust.

I decide to give the place half an hour, little knowing I'll devote the entire day to what awaits me — the world's most bizarre museum, forgotten and neglected to the point of sur-reality. The Soviets gave it that dull 'museum of ethnography' title. It began its existence as Peter the Great's *wunderkammer* or cabinet of wonders. When I first heard this term, years ago now, it reminded me of my innocent sense of things as a child, that the world was a wonderful place, full of marvels to be discovered, and indeed this is a childish version of the sense in which *wunderkammers* were regarded.

Peter conceived it in 1698 as the crowning jewel of Vasilevsky Island, which he planned as the intellectual centre of St Petersburg. Prominent in St Petersburg literature — particularly in the atmospheric writings of Pushkin, Dostoevski and Gogol — Vasilevsky Island, with its spires and turrets, is clearly visible across the broad choppy waters of the Neva from the embankment fronting the Hermitage and the Admiralty.

I'm approaching the *wunderkammer* now, from furiously busy Dvortsovy Bridge, with its screeching cable cars and darting pedestrians. Before me is a splendid panorama of classical buildings, their lustre dulled only by the centuries. Vasilevsky Island is, in a sense, like a map of Peter's seventeenth century mind and royal interests, its buildings — forts, academies, libraries, museums — reflecting his numerous passions. The pale blue and white *wunderkammer*, the oldest building on the island, dominates the left embankment. In spite of its now bedraggled air, it's obvious why, on its completion in 1726, a French traveller described it as 'the most beautiful building in Europe'.

Exotic statues add poetry to the grandeur of the scene before me. A famous pair of Egyptian sphinxes, said to be 3500 years old, guards the embankment fronting the Academy of Arts. Winged ships' angels on a towering maritime rostral

column are silhouetted darkly against the sky. And atop the dome of the *wunderkammer* itself sits the mystical symbol of the stargazer Ptolemy's earth-centred solar system — a golden armillary sphere. These magical emblems speak of an age when knowledge was associated with romance: Egypt's dark forgotten mysteries; the adventures of navigating uncharted oceans; the unfathomable laws of the cosmos. This sense of knowledge as wonderful, mystical almost, is the spirit in which Peter the Great conceived his museum.

I find the entrance to the *wunderkammer* in a side street. The panelled door swings open at my touch and I enter an abandoned world of marble staircases and chequered floors. Forms emerge like apparitions from the gloom: an Aztec god with petrified eyes, an African giant brandishing a club, a fabulous leopard with shark's killer teeth and a necklace of stag antlers — some taxidermist's joke, surely. Yes, but this step into the past is enough for me to recapture that sense of the marvellous I had as a child and the sensation of excitement that went with it. I have a premonition, as I do on rare occasions in museums or junk shops, that I will find something extraordinary here, something that will speak to me, a Medusa head, or a statue with an eternal look, as de Chirico would say.

A roaring Sumatran tiger leaps above me as I cross the sunless foyer to pay the entrance fee. All of the exhibits are thick with dust, yet they seem infinitely more alive than the morose attendant.

An equally surly babushka dogs my passage through the labyrinthine interior. Down endless corridors I enter silent rooms with exquisitely embroidered silks in dusty cases. In dimly lit halls stand towering eighteenth century vitrines of forgotten specimens. Barbaric gold jewellery from prehistoric Siberian tombs glistens on faded velvets. I pass ancient dioramas with cracked mannequins dressed in once-flamboyant ethnic costumes. Long ago these formed part of the ethnographic collection of the Dutch pharmacist Albertus Seba, whose famed cabinet of curiosities and natural wonders was one of the many great collections Peter purchased in its entirety for his *wunderkammer*. The Japanese gentleman on my right sitting down to a gelatinous lunch of king prawns and trout with nuts has done so since before European settlement of Australia. So has his neighbour, an Eskimo preparing a fish trap. In the native American diorama a Sioux warrior runs, spear upraised, at a stuffed bison, reminding me that Peter sent emissaries on collecting expeditions to places as remote as California and other parts of the New World. This is what fascinates me about this museum, the insights it gives into the mind of Russia's greatest ruler.

These rooms are deserted. What visitors there are have gravitated to the architectural heart of the museum, a beautiful circular room shaped like an anatomy theatre, with oval peepholes in its domed ceiling. This room is far better kept than the others for here in gleaming vitrines is displayed the one thing that people come here to see: the collection of preserved monsters assembled over fifty years by Professor Frederick Ruysch and sold to Peter the Great as the most wonderful collection of its kind.

It's a strange world, but it was far, far stranger before medical science cleaned it up. Most of these little creatures — two-headed calves, an eight-legged sheep with four eyes, two-headed babies, a duck-billed baby, a human frog — were killed soon after birth.

The word 'monster' historically refers to a malformed infant. Monstrous children and animals — teratologia — once had close associations with the wonderful as they belonged to the worlds of myth and magic. In Nineveh, for example, such infants were regarded as communications from the gods. In Egypt, too, they were held sacred: the gods Ptah and Bes were achondroplastic dwarfs, and an Egyptian queen and her daughter, both with achondroplasia, are depicted on a temple relief near Thebes. 'Nature,' wrote Pliny the pagan Roman, 'creates monsters for the purpose of astonishing us and amusing herself.'

With the onset of Christianity the picture darkened for these strange little creatures. They came to be regarded as sinful rather than sacred, as the offspring of the devil, and they and their mothers were accordingly put to death. Over the fifty years Professor Ruysch was assembling his collection, debate continued to rage as to whether teratologia were created by nature or the devil. Science entered the picture in the mid seventeenth century — at the outset of Ruysch's career — when the controversy shifted to whether the malformations were 'predicted' in the egg or whether they happened afterwards, due to the egg not developing correctly. By this stage their status as 'useful and interesting' specimens was fully established and the death sentence for malformed humans and animals in the name of science virtually guaranteed.

Within this circular theatre certain little faces in their glass jars stand out like masks of tragedy, expressing anything from resignation to agony and terror. The most striking is the angel-foetus Zabolotsky elegised in his poem. Ugly as he is — bulbous-faced, cauliflower-eared, malformed — he is the perfect expression of yearning. Even the larger, more bizarre exhibits in other vitrines are engaging not so much for their freakishness as for some moving quality, Eliot's infinitely gentle, infinitely suffering thing. The most poignant of all these poignant little creatures is not human. He's a dog, a tiny tan and white puppy. But for the fact that his head has been severed just above his chest and stitched back on, he is unblemished, perfect. He stares up as if at an intractable master, pleading for mercy.

A black infant's copious crinkly raven hair is arranged about her like mermaids' tresses. Her neighbour, also black, sits cross-legged, withdrawn like a miniature Buddha into a silent eternity of meditation. The deformities of these two, if they have any, are hidden. I suspect they were 'collected' for their black skin.

The longer I look at the scores of aberrant foetuses and infants floating in their formaldehyde worlds, the more I become aware of an invisible presence having stage-managed them. The human frog clutches his torso as if he's shivering with cold. The cabbage-patch-doll-faced baby with the aureole of fine golden hair presses her face against the glass: Let me out. The frowning infant whose body has been folded in half to fit it into the jar flinches back with its hand over its face as if warding off a blow. Mummified Siamese twins lie in an eternal embrace, arms entwined, one kissing her howling other on the cheek.

In one vitrine in particular the extent of Ruysch's involvement with these infant beings becomes more evident: a baby's amputated foot is adorned with a lace frill; tiny severed heads wear lace-edged lawn caps; an ivorine foetus with an empty sack for a body is arranged so as to contemplate his own insides — the spongy mass of organs and intestines is like some coral ocean floor.

After years of performing anatomical dissections on these beings, preserving them in spirit with black pepper, and then adding them to the collection he kept in open display cabinets in the rooms of his home, Frederick Ruysch began to marry science with art. The art of the day, the baroque, with its emphasis on distorted form and exaggerated ornament, suited his subjects perfectly. Like the pearl tears on Spanish Madonnas, it's not the monsters in this collection that are macabre but Ruysch's embellishing and arranging of them to maximum emotional effect. The monsters may be strange, but Ruysch himself is far, far stranger, for what comes across in all this is that the professor who hacked these infants to pieces and then sewed them up again had an affectionate attachment to them.

Peter the Great met Professor Ruysch on his formative trip to Europe in 1698, a meeting that was to prove inspirational in establishing his *wunderkammer*. Ruysch was the most renowned anatomist of his day, a pioneer in techniques of preserving organs and tissue who'd been appointed royal physician to the Dutch court. Peter attended one of Ruysch's famous anatomy lessons in Amsterdam, saying later, 'I saw at the doctor's the anatomy and all the innards were open. I saw the heart and the kidney. It was very wonderful.'

By the early seventeenth century the science of anatomy had become so popular in Amsterdam that physicians performed night dissections in anatomy theatres as paid public entertainment. These demonstrations were highly theatrical, performed by candlelight to the accompaniment of chamber music, some anatomists alluding to dissection's hallowed status as scientific revelation by reciting poems by antique authors as they worked.

A painting by Rembrandt, *The anatomy lecture of Doctor Nicolaas Tulp* (1632), shows a circle of men around a cadaver, looking on as Tulp dissects the arm. It's one of scores of seventeenth century Dutch pictures that depict dissections, and among them, yes, is one commemorating the work of Professor Ruysch — and this is where things get interesting.

Anatomies carried a powerful moral message, similar to the *vanitas* paintings — allegorical still lifes — then popular in

Holland: all things are subject to corruption and must die. With public dissections, the cadaver was that of an executed criminal provided by the law courts. Thus anatomists and the science of anatomy not only confronted death and gained insight into God's miracles, they triumphed over the ignorance of sin and elicited good from the lifeless body of an evildoer. Anatomists were indeed chosen ones, agents of revelation as well as healers of the sick.

The notable difference between *The anatomy lesson of Doctor Ruysch* (Jan van Nek, 1683) and other anatomy paintings is that the cadaver is a baby — not a 'monster' but an intact, healthy-looking baby. Following standard procedure, Ruysch has just completed his dissection of the abdominal cavity; the baby's intestines lie to one side. On the other lies the placenta, which one of the doctors gestures to. The umbilical cord is still attached to it and Ruysch holds up the long cord to see how far inside the baby it goes. To the right of the picture is another departure from the norm, to us a rather chilling one — Ruysch's rosy-cheeked son, who looks to be about ten, displays before him on a plinth the tiny skeleton of an infant: it grins as it performs a *danse macabre* — a reference to Ruysch's artworks.

A genius makes connections other people don't and the two things Ruysch brought together were more disparate even than the Surrealists' 'fortuitous encounter of an umbrella and a sewing machine on a dissecting table'. (The coincidence of the end of that famous sentence with the topic at hand is remarkable but meaningless.) What Ruysch fused into one seamless, extraordinary whole were the science of anatomy and *vanitas* painting. What he created were science's *vanitas* masterpieces.

Ruysch's creations were so original he popularised the use of a word remarkably similar to his own name. 'To ruche' means to gather or pleat fabric into a decorative frill. The noun 'ruche' describes one of these frills on a garment or article of soft furnishing. What Ruysch ruched, however, were the human body parts of infants and foetuses. Ruching was one of many techniques he deployed in the creation of his gruesome artworks, assembled as heavenly reminders of the power of the greatest artist of all, God, the creator of the human body:

> *How artists all are put to shame*
> *By the artful human frame*

Ruysch had a particular love of veins, which he described as 'God's very interesting drawings'. A pioneer in techniques of preservation, the preparation of raw materials for his assemblages involved draining veins and other organs of fluid, drying them, and then filling them with mercury or bees-wax, which also acted as colourants, the mercury imparting a silver glow.

Building up from a hexagonal timber base, he constructed elaborate fantastical gardens, the treated capillaries, arteries and veins forming leafy trees and exotic succulents, gallstones shaping rock gardens and grottoes, dried bladders and

stomachs fashioned into elegant vase and urn forms. Lastly he peopled this visceral paradise with characters — foetal skeletons — performing various witty antics. One of his more elaborate assemblages has a musical theme: the central skeleton plays a violin and his grinning offsider a set of drums while their festively plumed companion performs a *danse macabre*. It's diabolically amusing but has at the same time a funereal air, for stretched out at the base of this towering arrangement is the tiniest skeleton, its fragility a poignant reminder of what we are in fact looking at. Ruysch's assemblages are effortlessly artful yet highly elaborate, utterly baroque; the fact that they are composed entirely of body parts seems almost inconceivable.

What did Ruysch himself feel about his masterpieces? Encapsulating Christian Europe's schizophrenic attitudes to the human body at this time, he referred to them in poems as both heavenly offerings to God's artistry and as 'creating flowers out of filth'. Insistently present in the poems too — like the insidious presence of death in a *vanitas* painting — is the message that death is a gift of the merciful creator. If Ruysch genuinely believed this, then he would have equated his own role as an agent of death with that of a bestower of mercy. A God-like role indeed.

Peter the Great reputedly paid a high price for Ruysch's collection of 2000 items when he purchased it in 1718. At this time teratologia were the height of fashion; indeed collections of monsters were a must for the royal collector and Peter added to this one by acquiring Russian examples of monstrous animals. In Russia malformed humans were not considered monsters but were especially loved, either because God had marked them or because nature, not the Devil, had made them that way. Peter, who had a predilection for the unusual in any case, delighted in surrounding himself with dwarfs and freakish companions at his many entertainments and drunken revelries.

Peter hovers on my right as I ascend the spiral stairs to his study at the top of the tower. The conqueror, he stands etched against a background of glowering sky and the maritime port of St Petersburg with its anchored ships. Dressed as the scholar-king, his ornate crown resting on a plinth beside him, he is attended by an allegory of wisdom, Minerva perhaps, who casts an adoring glance at his handsome, dissipated face. At his feet lie scattered symbols of his dominion: a stack of thick volumes, hieroglyphic renderings, a tribal warrior's ermine-fringed drum. He rests one foot on a metal manuscript cylinder while a telescope balances against his left thigh. Tsardom is authority, beauty, world travel, the spoils of plunder, the accoutrements of knowledge, the oceans and heavens and divine approval.

Peter the Great must have felt as close to divine as it is possible for a human to feel, particularly one as earthy as he was. In 1698, knowing that Russia was still in many respects medieval, he set off on his tour of Europe's more enlightened capitals to bring himself — and ultimately Russia — up to date with the latest developments in science and other branches of knowledge. He was the first tsar ever to leave Russia.

Although on his formative trip abroad Peter was in many respects like a deprived child let loose in a gigantic toy factory, he shared with his more sophisticated European hosts an Enlightenment faith in knowledge and a sense of wonderment at the curious workings of the world. This seventeenth century preoccupation with the wonderful gave rise to the *wunderkammer*, hugely popular in Holland during Peter's visit. Peter returned to Russia determined to establish his own cabinet of wonders under the direction of his friend, the philosopher Leibniz. He wished it to be the most wonderful of them all, a microcosm of the world, and thus began his life's passion for collecting.

Peter also learnt things of vital significance on this eighteen month trip abroad, gleaning knowledge that equipped him to defeat the Swedes, to transform primitive Russia into a world power, and to create a glittering metropolis on a remote stretch of swampland in little more than a decade. By the end of his reign St Petersburg was known as the

Palmyra of the North. Fusing Peter and his city into a mythic entity, Pushkin described St Petersburg's miraculous birth as if it surfaced, fully formed, from the waves like Neptune's half-man, half-dolphin son:

> *And Petropolis surfaced like Triton*
> *Submerged in water to his waist*

Peter named the city after his patron saint, St Peter, and by 1712 he'd bullied the aristocracy into moving there from Moscow and declared it Russia's capital. Peter wasn't the first Russian ruler to obliterate the country's past and superimpose a new order upon it, and he certainly wouldn't be the last. It's a Russian habit.

In both personality and appearance Peter was the stuff of myth: he was nearly seven feet tall. Yet there was at the same time something common and workman-like about him. He delighted in disguising himself as a commoner on his travels; his favourite occupation was shipbuilding; he took as his wife an orphaned peasant girl, and engaged as his trusted lieutenant the pastry-cook Menshikov, elevating him to one of the highest positions in the empire.

What fascinates me most about Peter the Great, however, is his sense of himself and his extraordinary relationship with the world. Here was a man with a consummate belief that he could, like some divine being, come to know and do just about anything and everything. His passion for *wunderkammers* —

where everything in the world is symbolically represented — therefore makes perfect sense.

Peter's sense of omnipotence was combined with a rare giftedness. History has given us innumerable monarchs with supreme powers, most of them dreary tyrants. Rarely have they displayed Peter's genius. He was a true Renaissance man, mastering everything from paper-making to establishing Russia's first newspaper, from carving in ivory and watch-making to beating the Swedes at their own war games. While, infamously, his vast power entitled him to place a tax on the very souls of his subjects (and their beards) to raise revenue for the building of St Petersburg, his interest in absolutely everything equipped him to pull out the teeth of those subjects as well. Yes, he also learnt dentistry.

I enter his enormous study. It's circular with a domed ceiling. Antique desks and bookcases are crowded with manuscripts, books, papers, maps, clocks, mirrors and calendars, the latter a reminder that Peter introduced the Gregorian calendar during his reign and modernised the Russian alphabet.

I find a portrait of Catherine, Peter's second wife, depicted as a homely, buxom beauty. Russian women adore the classic Cinderella story of Catherine, the orphaned Livonian peasant girl Peter made tsarina of all the Russias. Although she is often characterised as a lowly servant who spent sixteen years as Peter's mistress before he defied his court and the Russian Orthodox Church to marry her, a fertile peasant who bore him eleven children, there was in reality something of the warrior queen about Catherine. She always accompanied Peter into battle, suffering unspeakable conditions for a woman in the freezing northern cold during interminable wars like the one with Sweden. A disastrous campaign — the Russian army surrounded by the Turkish one — was brought to an end when Catherine gave her jewels to bribe the Turks for terms of peace favourable to Russia. So it's not entirely incongruous that Peter, who was so in love with knowledge, should have loved a woman who was illiterate.

Instruments speak of Peter's numerous other interests: the astrolabes and globes of exploration; the phials and flasks of chemistry; the telescopes of astronomy; the geometric devices of architecture, and other antique implements whose strange uses are unknown to me. An ancient press may be the one that printed Russia's first newspaper, the *St Petersburg News*, founded by Peter in 1711. He kept tight control over its content, favouring news on public works in St Petersburg and reports on the latest shipment of monsters. Heavy censorship is a habit of centuries in Russia.

In an intimate niche I find a display of teeth extracted by Peter, along with items he made which show his mastery of various crafts — a watch, a model eye and ear carved from ivory, a tobacco box from bone, a carafe from a coconut, a vase from an elk's hoof.

I wonder how many of these hundreds of items were in his actual study, for the real one was in his Summer Palace on the Fontanka; this is an imagined one. Peter did not live to see the completion of his cabinet of wonders. Although building commenced in 1714, it dragged on for over twelve years until 1726, probably because Peter engaged three architects — Italian, French and Russian. Peter died unexpectedly in 1725, at the age of fifty-three, from complications resulting from a chill after he dived into the icy sea to rescue some sailors whose boat had capsized. It took a further two years to install Peter's collections and his *wunderkammer* finally opened to the public in 1728.

For the next twenty years it remained intact, the encyclopaedic world Peter had envisaged, where, as he'd wished, 'the people could look and learn'.

Outside, the sun emerges from a cloud and light streams through the window onto the golden orb of that most ancient and mystical of all astronomical devices — an armillary sphere. It resembles the one on the exterior of the building, except that this one stands on an elaborate wooden mount, the concentric criss-crossing circles of its planetary paths describing a spherical network around the gilded centre of its solar system — Earth. Across the room I see others — Peter must have had a passion for them.

The hands on his Dutch horizontal clock move eternally toward the middle of the day. I feel a great sense of privilege. Time has passed this place by. It knows nothing of the modern world, nothing of the Revolution or glasnost. Much of St Petersburg is ossified in the past, but nothing so completely as this museum. I have walked in here at a unique moment, at the tail end of more than two centuries of neglect. Tourism in St Petersburg is beginning to thrive. Very soon worthy officials or museologist types will raise their hands in horror at the forgotten state of Peter the Great's Museum of Ethnography and one of the world's most eccentric and historically intact museums will be lost forever.

RASKOLNIKOV ON A WHITE NIGHT

An official wants Tamara's apartment, so she's going to have to get out. For a woman who's just informed me she'll be murdered if she doesn't, she's strangely calm and stubborn. Her contempt for the situation eclipses all else. They have found her a substitute apartment in the high-rise wasteland on the fringes of the city.

'Who are *they*?' I ask.

She gestures disdainfully, as if she's flicking off a spider. 'I will not live in this terrible place. They must show me the apartment in the centre.'

'But what if they don't? What will you do?'

She shrugs.

For Tamara not to live in the historical centre of St Petersburg is unthinkable. Because of her work, the history of this city, its culture and artists — living and dead — are the focus of her life. Like lovers, she and the city belong to each other.

Yet it's inevitable that ordinary St Petersburgers will be forced out of the centre, which is attracting increasing numbers of tourists. The city's vice-governor, Mikhail Manevich, has been in the news a lot lately for the extraordinary fact that he is widely considered to be an honest and innovative politician, bent on instituting reforms to tackle the corruption and mafia elements associated with the rent rackets. At the moment in Russia, no central government policies have been handed down to effect the transition from state to private ownership of property. The chaos of the situation has enabled criminal elements to seize control of the property and rental markets. Manevich insists that basic laws like tenancy laws must be upheld.

'Would it help if you wrote to Manevich?' I ask Tamara.

She grimaces. 'What can he do?'

'Isn't he dealing with situations like yours? Trying to stop criminals from controlling housing?'

She looks at me as if I'm an idiot. The naïve Australian. 'They are all criminals.'

'Manevich too?'

'Maybe not,' she says flatly. It's impossible for her to have any faith in a politician. As she has pointed out to me several times, Russians don't understand democracy. They've never experienced it, so they don't know how it works.

As she rummages in spilling cupboards with a preoccupied frown — her usual expression — I clear our tea things from the tiny cluttered table and make for the hallway. She stops me. Tamara is so ashamed of the squalid kitchen with its six stoves she shares with the occupants of seven other apartments, she hates me going in there.

'Please let me help, Tamara. Anyway, I want to use the toilet.'

Her frown deepens. The shared toilet is even more embarrassing than the kitchen and bathroom. She finds a rough toilet roll and hands it to me, saying '*Tak!*' (So!) an expression she regularly mutters distractedly to herself.

Balancing the crockery and toilet roll I shuffle in her slippers — too big for me — to the drab foyer with its ragged carpet and neat rows of shabby shoes and coats on hooks, and step out of the slippers and into my red rubber shoes. I find the Russian custom of wearing slippers in the house irksome. Why bother when the floors are so dirty? It's a snow-country habit.

The gloomy corridor is silent. I hold my breath as I pass the toilet. Reaching the kitchen I deposit the china on the side of the sink I know is Tamara's; its white porcelain coating has all but worn away, leaving an abrasive brown surface. I once attempted to wash the dishes here but turning on the tap produced no water, only a loud shuddering in the pipes which brought Tamara rushing to the scene, so now I don't bother. The dingy kitchen with its ancient grease is curiously tidy: eight neat clusters of food and cooking utensils arranged on ugly tables. No cupboards, no chairs, no exhaust fan; only a narrow window with a fragment of curtain, its glass opaque with dirt. The lino, colour unidentifiable, is worn down to its hessian backing in the centre.

Something scrabbles under one of the ancient stoves and I almost run out.

I take a deep breath — can I hold it for the time it takes to piddle? — and rush into the lavatory. I straddle the seatless toilet, knees bent, terrified of my body coming into contact with such disgusting filth. (On my return to Australia, I discover, to my horror, I've caught four different kinds of worms anyway, but this is probably due to the indescribable public toilets.) I finish and stretch up on tiptoe to pull what remains of the chain. It doesn't flush. In spite of myself I look into the bowl. It hasn't been cleaned for years and is so repulsively poop-brown it's vilely fascinating; blobs of someone else's shit float in the water. I have to breathe, so the foul stench hits my nostrils. At least I don't gag this time.

The windowless bathroom stinks of the mildew that patterns the ceiling and walls. Eight clusters of cheap soap and toothbrushes, some with toothpaste, line up along a rough wooden plank slung across the remains of a medicine cabinet. I recognise Tamara's Imperial Leather and quickly wash my hands and shake them dry. I've showered twice in this bathroom now — careful not to touch the surfaces — so I know the cold tap actually works.

Back in the haven of Tamara's apartment I feel my shoulders relax. I breathe in the faintly vanilla smell that hangs in the room as I soothe my assaulted senses with the sight of her books, her paintings, the high baroque ceiling and tall windows with the fashionable street beyond. She has finally found the jacket she wants to wear — olive-green mock suede — and is combing her shoulder-length brown hair in front of a plastic mirror propped against a stack of papers on the chipped grand piano.

She has to move so I can squeeze past to get my new Russian handbag. It cost 18,000 rubles (eight dollars) and I love its capaciousness, its classic Gladstone shape, its shiny grey plastic. I bought it yesterday in Nevsky Prospekt at Gostiny Dvor, the colonnaded Florentine-style department store — more an assortment of market stalls. Ada thought I was crazy to prefer it to my Italian leather one. 'Russia make you have the bad taste,' she said disapprovingly.

———•◦•———

It's ten p.m. Outside, the sky glows pearly white.

'This is so exciting,' I say.

Tamara smiles. 'Peterbourg has made the white night just for you. It is too late in the er ...' She purses her generous mouth, searching the room for the word.

'Season?'

'Season for the white sky. But it comes this night. *Tak.* We go?'

We cross crowded Nevsky Prospekt, passing under the bronze hooves of the magnificent rearing horses on the bridge across the Fontanka, and turn left along the Griboedova Canal.

We're heading for the Sennaya Ploshchad district — Dostoevski country. Tamara waves away my guidebook; she knows Raskolnikov's murderous route in *Crime and Punishment*.

'We take the long way,' she says with a mysterious air.

I'm thinking how St Petersburg with its network of canals and bridges is rightly called the Venice of the North — even though it is a city of grand prospects, rather than intimate like Venice — when a highly elaborate little wrought-iron footbridge comes into view.

'Oh Tamara, let's cross it.'

'Of course.' She's watching me, smiling. 'The Bankovsky Bridge she is so *beautiful*, yes?'

'The most beautiful I've ever seen,' I say, meaning it. 'It's magical.'

We cross it, my eyes glued to the pair of mythical creatures towering at the other end — enormous black griffins with golden wings, staring down at us like sentinels to another world.

We pass between them and follow the canal's meandering course, Tamara pointing out the dwellings of long-dead artists, writers and musicians among the handsome classical buildings.

We stand admiring the exquisite sky-blue and white cathedral of St Nicholas. Tamara tells me of the priest who sheltered hundreds of people here during the Siege of Leningrad.

'You had priests here after the Revolution? I thought the Soviets outlawed religion.'

She makes a dismissive *pfff* sound. 'The Soviets they outlaw everything. The priests are always in Russia.'

'But weren't thousands of them executed?'

'They come back. Stalin blows up the churches but he can't kill the religion. He pushes it — what is it in English? — under the ground.'

'Underground.'

I look up at the iridescent sky; there is no illusion of a canopy as with a blue sky; only weightless, atomless mother-of-pearl light, a heavenly absence of colour. The golden domes of the cathedral float in space. I stare at Tamara's beautiful face, hardly hearing what she's saying. I'm amazed at the faintly roseate aura that clings to her, softening her features. Her tired skin looks young, dewy. I look around and see that everybody is wrapped in this ethereal radiance. I've stumbled onto a surreal stage set where the movements of the crowd are the subtlest of theatrical performances.

As soon as we make a U-turn into Sadovaya Ulitsa the landscape begins to shift, princely architecture giving way to seedy old tenement buildings with gloomy courtyards. I remember Mitri saying this was a 'bad area'. Tamara takes my arm, steering me around a gaping hole in the potholed pavement. The city has no money for public works.

Before I know what's happening a man lurching toward us grabs my breast and lurches on. I stand stupefied, feeling the blood rush to my face. Tamara shouts at him; he turns and pulls a stupid, leering face, teetering drunkenly and waving his arms about. Angry now, I stick my tongue out and gesture rudely. Tamara grabs my arm. 'No, no, you must not do this. You make him come back. Say something in English, quick.'

'Fucking ugly arsehole,' I yell.

The effect is miraculous. His face sags with remorse and he makes an attempt at a bow, muttering something imploringly.

'What's he saying?'

'He ask you to forgive him. He do it because you are beautiful and he must touch you. He think you are Russian.'

'Okay, piss off, Marmeladov,' I yell. He reminds me of Sonia's drunken, obsequious father in *Crime and Punishment*.

Tamara says something to him and he staggers off like a mangy dog. She turns to me, mortified. 'Vika, I am so sorry. Such a terrible thing ...'

'It's all right, Tamara. Really, I'm all right. There are idiots like that all over the world.'

It suddenly strikes me as funny. 'How could someone so drunk have such perfect aim?' I laugh.

Tamara doesn't think it's funny; she shakes her head mournfully. How much more dignified she is than I am, I think, wondering if she understood the abuse I shouted at him.

This is Dostoevski country all right.

———•◦•———

We arrive at Ulitsa Przhevlskogo (Dostoevski's 'S ... Lane') and enter a dark tunnel, the gateway to No 9. We emerge into a dim courtyard with two entrances and Tamara heads straight for the one on the right. A little tabby cat mewing plaintively at the other entrance runs toward us and I hesitate. Tamara gives me a warning look so after a quick pat I follow her into the gloom and up crumbling stone steps. The air smells earthy, damp. At the top of the fourth flight I look up at the slanted ceiling — Raskolnikov's attic must be just above us.

'Tamara.'

She turns to face me. 'Yes.'

'It's just like in the book.'

She laughs. 'I told you this. You don't believe me?'

'Yes, of course I do, but it's hard to believe it could be the same after so long. When did he write *Crime and Punishment*?'

'1860.'

'That's a hundred and forty years ago,' I say, amazed.

'You see? Russia has the revolution and the perestroika and nothing change for the people. Only get worse. Come, we go up.'

As we reach the fifth floor my amazement increases. On the wall in large red graffiti are the words — in English — DON'T DO IT RODYA. And below it in blue — RODYA, DON'T KILL. (Rodya is the familiar of Rodyon — Raskolnikov's first name.)

'This is his room,' says Tamara, pointing to a padlocked door.

For some weird reason I walk across and knock on it, pressing my ear against the door and listening. Tamara seems to think this is perfectly normal. Silence.

We emerge from the gloomy building and follow the circuitous route Raskolnikov took to the old pawnbroker's. Opposite the Yusupov Palace we lean over the elaborate railing to look at the spot in the canal where the legendary Rasputin finally met his icy death. It seems strange to me now to learn that the 'holy fool' was only poisoned, shot in the head, heart and back, and drowned in the canal. The highly exaggerated accounts I'd been enthralled by as a teenager claimed he'd been repeatedly stabbed and bludgeoned as well. Even stranger are recent claims that Prince Yusupov was not Rasputin's assassin. It seems that everything, even the most incontrovertible of facts, is now being questioned in Russia.

A few minutes later we stand at another bridge railing,

looking into the dirty water of the Kokushkin Canal. Tamara tells me this is the very spot where Raskolnikov would often stop to think and gaze into the canal. It strikes me that Raskolnikov — a fictional character — is as real to her as Rasputin — a historical figure. But then I remember the graffiti outside his room — it's not only Russians Raskolnikov is real to. Youth everywhere loves him because he represents anarchy; mature fans respond to him more as a figure of repentance and remorse, and sociologist types see him as the symbolic victim of poverty driven to crime. You can't get much more universal than that.

Several twists and turns later we finally reach the old pawnbroker's and stand on Komsomolsky Bridge looking at the building which sits between Srednyaya Podacheskaya and the canal embankment. We cross the street, enter another dank tunnel and mount three flights of stairs to the pawnbroker's flat. Here the line between reality and fiction becomes further blurred. Three brass balls — pawnbrokers' symbols — sit on the corners of the iron banisters.

'Does a real pawnbroker actually live here?' I ask Tamara.

'No,' she says, a little puzzled. 'This is for the visitors who look for the apartment of the pawnbroker Raskolnikov murder.'

'Ah!' (What a backward child I am.)

These are the very steps Raskolnikov mounted and descended in his frenzy. On the third floor, outside the pawnbroker's door, I think of the bloody murder of the old pawnbroker and her half-witted sister Lizaveta, still the most frenzied murder in literature. Why is it so memorable? Because of its sheer senselessness. It's so modern. Raskolnikov is about to be thrown out of his lodgings and he deals with the situation by committing murder.

I wonder how Tamara will deal with her housing situation. I wonder if it could really happen as she says — that she'll be murdered if she doesn't comply. It doesn't seem possible.

———•—•———

The next morning — unbelievable that it could be the very next day, but there you are, fact is stranger than fiction — I'm strolling down Nevsky Prospekt. I've just looked at some lustrous black cultured pearls in the splendid nineteenth century arcaded department store, Passazh. I hear gunshots — several rapid reports, loud and clear. The air's electric with incident. Jolted, I stand stock-still and listen. The shots sounded as if they came from about two blocks away. Should I run? Panic? I listen for reactive sounds, screams or sirens. Nothing. Just ordinary city noises, as if the shots never happened. Unnerved, I cross the street and crane my neck, looking south toward the Hermitage. Two blocks away the corner of the wonderful art nouveau Singer building — now St Petersburg's finest bookshop — is clearly in view. Everything seems normal. No one else has stopped or crossed the road.

The crowd up ahead continues walking. There are no cries or running figures. I must have been mistaken. One of those beat-up Russian cars must have backfired.

I return to Passazh and buy the black pearls for an unbelievable 35,000 rubles (16 dollars).

———•·•———

The next day I'm having coffee in the ritzy bar of the plush Hotel Europa. Coffee is all I can afford here but I come regularly because of the hotel's breathtaking art nouveau interiors and because I can pick up a copy of the *St Petersburg Times* and catch up on the news.

MANEVICH ASSASSINATED ON NEVSKY PROSPEKT runs the headline.

Yesterday at 11.34 a.m. Vice-Governor Mikhail Manevich was murdered when his Volvo turned slowly into stately Nevsky Prospekt. Eight bullets from an AK-47 pierced the car's roof and front window. Five struck Manevich, 36, in the neck and chest, and he died before reaching hospital.

'It's hard to think about progress in a place where a chief city manager is struck down by bullets on the main street,' said Alexander Belyayev, an economist and businessman.

'Of course, this killing raises the question of whether law and order can take hold in Russia,' said Igor

Artemyev, the city's Finance Committee chairman and a close colleague of Manevich ...

In recent months, Manevich received threats from organised crime gangs, acquaintances say. Nonetheless, he habitually travelled at normal road speed in an unarmoured Volvo, with no security escort and no sirens blaring to disperse traffic ...

'What he was trying to do was make it unimportant who was dealing in property, that what counted was the law,' said German Graf, Manevich's successor at City Hall.

'It was a demonstration murder. They could have killed him on his front doorstep or somewhere else. They wanted to make a point.'

So it *was* gunshots I heard yesterday. I'm stunned, shocked that events could take such an obvious course. No room for subtle plot deviations in this place.

I'm so agitated I think of rushing across to the Russian Museum to discuss it with Tamara right now, even though I'm seeing her tonight. But then I decide not to, anticipating her fatalistic shrug. Tamara always expects the worst.

Cold creeps up my spine. If Tamara always expects the worst, why is she openly defying these murderous bastards? If they can kill Manevich in broad daylight in St Petersburg's busiest street, disposing of Tamara would be like extinguishing a flame. I picture her with them, her haughty face expressing her utter contempt. How they must hate her.

———•———

That night I express these thoughts to her. She remains so strangely calm, I ask, 'Would you rather die than be pushed around by these people? Have you reached that point?'

'Of course not,' she replies. 'They will find me an apartment in the centre.'

'How can you possibly know that?'

'Because they must.'

Like Manevich, she's refusing to change her behaviour. No, it's more than that. The situation is beginning to distance her from reality — she's becoming a little crazy.

PALACE OF ILLUSIONS

———◆———

On an airless afternoon in June 1941 Tatiana, a worker at
Pavlovsk Palace, sat hurriedly sketching the intricate folds of a
heavy curtain in the boudoir of Maria Feodorovna, wife of the
ill-fated Tsar Paul I. The room looked onto an intimate garden
with parterres and spilling urns of roses. Through the boudoir's
long windows Tatiana was half-aware of moving figures in this
garden, darting back and forth carrying sculptures and statuary.
Elsewhere in the vast palace her comrades were packing and
crating its treasures to be sent north, to Novosibirsk in Siberia.
Bigger statues were being buried in underground crypts or large
holes they'd dug in the grounds. For two months their days had
been devoted to this work, and would continue to be for
another month.

Tatiana finished her sketch, one of twenty she made
documenting the pleats and scallops of Pavlovsk's draperies
and hangings. She snatched time to do this in between packing
the tapestries and costumes in her care. Her concern was

this: *if the unthinkable happened, who would later know, who would remember, the vagaries of these elaborate arrangements?*

Tatiana walked through sumptuous rooms and up a marble staircase to the library on the top floor, modelled on the legendary Gonzaga library at Urbino. She stood at the tall windows and looked down at the manicured gardens and surrounding park, now littered with sandbags and gaping holes. In the distance she could see the rose pavilion built to commemorate Russia's defeat of Napoleon — how festive and enchanting it was.

Tatiana did not tell her comrades of her fervent admiration for Maria Feodorovna or how privileged she felt to work at beautiful Pavlovsk. While it was the duty of the staff of tsarist palaces — now museums — to care for them so that Russia's history could be interpreted to the people, any enthusiasm would inevitably be misconstrued and reported. She'd once shared her love of beautiful things with her fiancé, a soldier, but he'd been killed long ago, in the civil war that followed the Revolution.

She often thought how ironic it was that the Revolution St Petersburg had given birth to had drained it of vigour, even stolen its identity as Russia's capital. Its very name had been taken — it was now called Leningrad. Since the Terror in particular, the city had become a shell of its former self. The only reminders of what it had once been were Pavlovsk and the other shimmering palaces on its outskirts: Peterhof, the showplace on the Gulf of Finland built by Peter the Great to rival Versailles, with its fantasia of fountains and cascading waters designed by Peter himself; Gatchina, Catherine the Great's gift to her lover Orlov, with its Island of Love and Temple of Venus; and the most ostentatiously magnificent of them all — Catherine's Tsarkoye Selo (Tsar's Village) and its jewel, Yekaterininsky dvordets — the Catherine Palace designed by the great Rastrelli.

On a summer night in July, just two days after the last of Pavlovsk's crates had been sent off to Novosibirsk, Tatiana lay in her bed in an apartment on the other side of the forest and heard German bombers mount Hitler's massive surprise attack on Russia. She hardly needed to rush to Pavlovsk early the next morning, as she did, to know that the palace had been reduced to a smouldering ruin. A few exterior walls were all that remained. News soon reached her that Peterhof, too, had been destroyed. Then Gatchina — flattened. And finally, Tsarskoye Selo. Gone. Was it possible? The immense Catherine Palace. Forever lost.

Tatiana lived to regret surviving Pavlovsk. Within two months the German Wehrmacht reached the outskirts of the city and surrounded it, and thus began the horrors of the 900 day Siege of Leningrad. Tatiana and her three pet dogs, strays she had long ago rescued, eked out a shaky existence on rations and handouts for nearly two years. Unable to bring herself to eat the rats or indeed dogs that became standard fare in the final months of the siege, and *horrified by the fixated stares of desperate neighbours at her pets, Tatiana barricaded herself in her apartment. There she and her loyal old dogs lay together on her big bed and silently succumbed to starvation.*

More than half a century after these events, Nadezha, a curator at Pavlovsk and friend of Ada and Tamara, is showing me Tatiana's drawings. We are standing in Maria Feodorovna's boudoir, its parterres and spilling urns of roses visible through the long windows, and I look from drawing to curtain and see that the pleats and scallops of the latter perfectly replicate the former. Nadezha has just shown me the library upstairs, proudly telling me it's modelled on the Duc de Gonzaga's Renaissance library at Urbino.

How is this possible? Am I dreaming? No. I really am at Pavlovsk and Pavlovsk is real. The palace has been completely reconstructed, right down to the elaborate detailing of its gold cornices and hand-painted ceilings, even its classical Italian and Grecian rooms entirely recreated. This has, of course, taken decades.

Nadezsha leads Ada and me outside. Crossing the formal garden and the park beyond we reach the reconstructed rose pavilion at the edge of the forest. We stand on an arched bridge over a babbling brook, admiring the wooden pavilion in its idyllic setting, and I have this curious sense of myself as a figure in one of those eighteenth century conversation piece paintings where idle aristocrats amuse themselves in

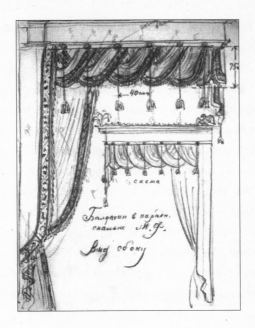

picturesque parks. Ermines and red squirrels make this park especially charming.

Ada and I titter ooh-so-amusedly at Nadezha's account of what happened this morning on this very spot. One of the curators, a young man, was chased through the forest by a wild boar and, on reaching the iron bridge, climbed to safety in one of its enormous ornamental urns, the boar grunting threateningly below. He remained there for most of the morning, his bottom lodged firmly in the urn, until rescued by a gardener with a rake.

Nadezha's so immersed in Pavlovsk's world she simply

takes my breath away. Is she even aware that the Russian Revolution took place?

Still, it's fair to say that this honey-blonde woman, handsome and assured, might well have been an aristocrat herself if she'd lived two centuries ago, a companion to her adored Maria Feodorovna, and I have the feeling that her work at Pavlovsk has overtones of escapist fantasy, time out at least, from her life in a cramped apartment with her much older, dour husband (Tsar Paul?) and his ancient mother. Nadezha's skin is grey, her large green eyes ringed with exhaustion. She lavishes affection on her two beautifully groomed dogs and, yes, the story she told me about Tatiana, her predecessor of half a century ago, is in a sense a story about herself as well.

We walk back through the grounds to her softly lit, three-room office on the ground floor of the palace, a curator's dream. Its tall antique chests of drawers contain all manner of neatly catalogued marvels. Reverentially she shows me the textiles in her care: fans of ivory and Brussels lace; impossibly heavy priestly vestments embroidered with silver thread; Maria Feodorovna's most beautiful court costume — cream silk scattered with lifelike hand-made roses; and a mannish outfit in apple-green moiré worn by Catherine the Great.

She opens a drawer and extracts a black Chantilly lace fan, excitedly telling me its iridescent black mother-of-pearl is Australian and that it once belonged to Maria Feodorovna. Through the window I look outside to the fading *trompe l'oeil* fresco, its painted columns joining with real columns in an architectural play on illusion and reality. This wall is one of the few that remain of the original palace and the only thing I really like about Pavlovsk: its quality as a palace of illusions.

Pavlovsk is not the only destroyed palace to have been resurrected. Peterhof and its 140 fountains have also been miraculously reconstructed. Most unbelievable of all, so has extravagant Tsarskoye Selo. Gatchina, too, has been rebuilt, although work on its interiors is not yet complete.

Who initiated this vast enterprise?

Stalin.

There's much in all this that I find puzzling and contradictory. Why did Stalin do this? He loathed St Petersburg. During the Terror in the thirties he deliberately destroyed its culture, so why recreate that culture's most glittering symbols, ones that were historical residences of the enemy, the tsars?

The attitude of my friends to these palaces — or, rather, copies of palaces — also intrigues me. Ada, Tamara and Nadezha revere them and one or the other has accompanied me to all of them and generously arranged for personal tours; we spend whole days at each, bombarded with tsarist narratives. It's clear the palaces are considered to be among the highlights of any visit to St Petersburg. So how could I ever tell them that, fascinated as I am by the architecture of the past, reconstructed palaces don't hold much allure for me, that for me the real beauty of historic buildings is interwoven with the passage of time, with the poignancy of stains and faded surfaces? Even the magnificence of Peterhof is a hollow experience, a mere reminder of what has been irretrievably lost.

In spite of this I am awestruck by the Russian mastery of historical reconstruction. Who could fail to be? Imagine rebuilding the Sun King's Versailles today, right down to its glittering interiors and extravagant setting with its cascading waters. This is the kind of staggering achievement we are dealing with. It is in itself a miracle that such artistry — associated, after all, with the tsars and aristocratic patronage — was kept alive during the Soviet period.

Ada and Tamara know all this; they have insiders' understanding of the craftsmanship, the sheer physical manpower, that makes these reconstructions possible. Yet when I express my amazement to them they look at me blankly. Indeed it's clear that, emotionally at least, they don't think of the palaces in terms of reconstructions at all: Pavlovsk is still the very Pavlovsk that Catherine the Great built in 1763 for her son Paul I, and so on. (Coincidentally most of these palaces don't draw attention to their status as reconstructions; most tourists think they're the real thing. The exception is Pavlovsk.) Why is this? I must tease out the answer because it will reveal — what? — something crucial about the lives of my friends that eludes me.

———•—•———

Toward the end of a long day at the vast Catherine Palace — yes, a miracle of baroque reconstruction where rooms of gold leaf and mirrors give the illusion of no walls — Tamara and I pause in the opium den, one of a cluster of rooms high in the palace devoted to pleasure and fantasy. (Did Catherine chase the dragon?) Glancing over its rich oriental interior designed for lolling about — each carpet, embroidery and furniture item a copy of a destroyed original — I experience a weird sense of unreality. What is the point of making copies down to the last frivolous detail of a world that is forever lost, not just lost in time but also physically destroyed? The weirdest angle is that individuals as diverse as Stalin and Tamara regard the rationale for this as self-evident.

How to broach this subject with Tamara?

'Do you think Hitler was trying to get at Stalin by bombing these palaces?' I ask her.

She treats me to one of her withering looks.

'It's just that it seems so personal, that early attack on the palaces. The destruction of such a large slice of Russia's cultural heritage in one campaign. Maybe Hitler did this to punish Stalin for going over to the Allies.'

'What would Stalin care about this palaces?' Tamara asks disdainfully.

'They must have mattered to him. He …'

'Why? Why would they matter to him? Ask yourself,' she says angrily.

'I don't know. Maybe because they're symbols of magnificence …'

'*Pffff,*' she sneers.

'Or Russian power,' I insist. 'I can't guess why. But they must have mattered to him. Otherwise, why would he have ordered them to be reconstructed?'

'Nobody know why Stalin do this,' she says with a dismissive flick of her hand.

I regret bringing this up. Ever the interested traveller, I sometimes forget that my friends have cares, which is certainly the case with Tamara at the moment. Each time I've asked her about the situation with her apartment, the tension in the air could have been cut with a knife, so I rarely mention it. When I ask Ada she shrugs; it seems she doesn't mention it either. And now I've thoughtlessly made Tamara angry. She doesn't like to be reminded that Stalin initiated the reconstructions. Neither do Ada and Nadezha. It's as if they don't wish the tsars' palaces to be tainted by an association with Stalin and other Soviet rulers. To overlook the status of the palaces as reconstructions is to retain their tsarist purity and deny Stalin his role, which goes to show how deep-seated their hatred of him is.

As each day passes some new event causes another aspect of my friends' mysterious attachments to unfold, not just the obsession with the palaces and half-denial of what they in reality are, but their reverence for the Romanovs. This extends even to the Tsars who were clearly deranged, like Paul I who spent his first day on the throne issuing a decree outlawing waistcoats. Their fascination is partly bound up with the Russian instinct for storytelling. Even sordid episodes in the tsars' lives are woven into a beguiling, charac-teristically Russian blend of history, fairytale and absurdity.

At the Mikhailovsky Palace Nadezha shows me Paul I's bedroom and the trapdoor to its secret staircase, which led to his mistress's apartment. If Paul needed to escape, she explains, he had only to tap hard with the heel of his shoe and the trapdoor would spring open. One fateful night he happened not to be wearing his shoes because he was in bed with his mistress, and the members of his court who broke down his door in order to assassinate him did so with ease, in spite of his hiding behind the fire screen. So far, it's standard tour-of-the-royal-castle storytelling. But then Nadezsha takes me into the room next door and tells me that on the night of his assassination, this is where Paul locked his wife Maria Feodorovna. She points to one of the exterior walls. 'You see this wall has no window?' she asks me. I nod. Her face takes on a dreamy cast. 'In eighteenth century this wall did have a window. Sometimes on certain nights, when you look up here from the outside, this wall has window still. And Maria Feodorovna and Paul I stand together at this window.'

My puzzlement as to why a woman whose husband locked her up while he was in bed with his mistress would want to stand beside him for all eternity is compounded by the fact the palace's interiors were in the nineteenth century completely refurbished in vile English neo-Gothic style, so nothing of Tsar Paul remains. In the next breath Nadezha tells me that this is where Dostoevski studied engineering and my befuddlement is complete.

To be honest, I'm sick to death of Maria Feodorovna. I've seen too many artificial palaces, too much of the past. Nobody here seems to remember that this now idealised past was in reality the tyrannical system which gave birth to the Revolution. What followed was so dark that the past is now remembered as a glorious sunset.

What I really crave is something contemporary. But it's not to be, not this week.

———— · ◦ · ————

I sit with Ada under the portico of a decaying Italianate pavilion in the gardens at Oranienbaum — Catherine the Great's pleasure palace — sheltering from the rain. In Catherine's time there was a roller-coaster here, which courtiers would fly down in little toboggans. Oranienbaum is truly beautiful, even to me. It is not a reconstruction; its buildings are original and their current state of fragility perfectly complements their rococo lightness and whimsy.

Ada says to me, 'I often think of Maria Feodorovna. You know, she had ten children to Paul and I do not think it is true what Nadezsha told you, that she was very friendly with his mistress.'

'Nadezsha's in love with the tsars and wants everything about their lives to be elegant,' I venture.

'It's true, it's true,' chirrups Ada, clapping her hands appreciatively. We laugh conspiratorially, although secretly I think that Nadezsha is not the only one in love with the tsars. Who wouldn't be captivated by such glamorous lives, such intriguing narratives of wealth, sex, madness and scandal, given the thumping dullness of the lives that replaced them?

We scamper across the park to view St Petersburg's most extravagant original interiors, in the Chinese Palace. Grim, apron-clad babushkas on the inside of the French doors gesture for us to wait outside in the pouring rain; they let in only so many visitors at a time, even though there are acres of foyer inside. Under Ada's umbrella we stand before pastel walls looking up at delicate iron balconies half obscured by lush creepers. Time passes and a queue forms.

The glass doors open at last and we're rudely herded inside and made to select a pair of ridiculously awkward felt-soled cloth shoes from a grubby heap. Wearing these prevents damage to the parquetry and, I suspect, makes floor cleaning unnecessary.

We stand for long minutes in an unremarkable reception room while the tour guide, a humourless apparatchik, delivers an interminable introductory speech in Russian. She's thirtysomething and not unattractive in a dominatrix kind of way, but she's like some KGB relic. How many *hours* of this will I have to endure?

At last she stiffly opens one of a pair of tall doors and impassively stands guard as we file through. Ada nudges me, reminding me not to speak. We've paid the Russian price for my ticket, so I can't divulge that I'm a foreigner or I'll have to pay twenty times that price. Literally.

But who wants to talk. What a room! What joyous rococo extravagance. What uplifting eroticism. On the ceiling a dishevelled Mars and Venus recline post-coitally, their cheeks still suffused with rosy warmth, their eyes still eyeing each other languorously across the room. Venus's exposed breast with its erect pink nipple is a perfect apple of lust; Mars' muscular thighs strain tumescently. With their draperies and cupid attendants, they float and swirl above us in a paradise of carnality.

The dour guide starts up a toneless monologue. She drones on and on.

I stand there looking up at the ceiling, thinking what pleasurable times Catherine the Great and Orlov must have had in this room. Presumably the two of them identified very strongly with the Mars and Venus on the ceiling. What an exciting, Machiavellian character Orlov must have been, organising his two brothers to murder Catherine's tedious husband so she could become tsarina. I smile to myself, caught out in my own bit of tsar-glorifying. But then women like Catherine who take matters into their own hands have always thrilled me.

The twenty occupants of the room have had their eyes glued to the ceiling for the last ten minutes and still the flat monologue drones on. What a contrast, the deadly earnestness of the guide's tone and the ecstasy of the images.

'What's she saying?' I whisper to Ada.

She kicks my foot to be quiet but can't resist whispering an answer. 'She tell about dates and owners and how Catherine promote French style in Russia.'

'What about the subject matter?' I whisper.

'She say nothing,' Ada whispers back, smiling.

We exchange glances bursting with suppressed laughter.

The apparatchik wraps up her speech and as she ushers us into the next room she flings Ada and me a look that would kill the birds in the trees stone dead.

'That guide is trained in Soviet style of presenting the tour,' says Ada to me as we walk to the bus stop along silent paths through pine woods. 'I think maybe now you appreciate Nadezsha's more recent style to make everything so interesting.'

Ah Ada, how perceptive you are.

———•◦•———

Strangely enough, it is Anatole, with whom I cannot converse, who brings home to me the full force of the sense of loss that is the source of what I'm arrogantly beginning to regard as my friends' denial of reality. He takes me to one of the most spectacular buildings of all — also partly destroyed during the Second World War — the St Petersburg School of Industrial Arts, where he is a senior lecturer. Founded by the Russian industrialist Baron Stieglitz in the 1870s, it is both a school of art and design, and a museum with a wealth of historical art collections, modelled on London's Victoria and Albert Museum. The innumerable halls and galleries of the building were designed to be instructive to students, so each is a dazzling recreation of great moments in western art, from classical Greek and Roman, through Byzantine and the Italian Renaissance to the French and German baroque.

Predictably, the afternoon begins with buffoonery but then more serious aspects of Anatole emerge: the aesthete and the teacher. On arrival, we stand in front of an antique Roman bust and he pretends to give me a serious lecture, parodying historical commentary — and, I suspect, the museum's pompous director who has just greeted us, told us how terribly busy he is and flown back to his office. Mimicking the stony expression of the bust, silently mouthing words and gesturing at its features, Anatole conveys to me its profound art historical significance, terminating the dumb show by wagging his finger in the air with the pronouncement, 'Classique.' I'm bursting with laughter and he sternly admonishes me. 'Classique,' he bellows, wagging his finger at my nose.

He takes me on a tour through marble halls to the school, showing me the classrooms where he teaches and introducing me as 'Arfstraalian critique' to a couple of his students, who seem to be very respectful and rather nervous of him.

He saves the best part for last — the Grand Exhibition Hall — but before we enter he shows me old photographs of its partial destruction by two German shells and a bomb, and a 1947 one of reconstruction work on its immense domed glass ceiling. He then leads me to one of its upstairs galleries and we stand looking down on the vast space itself, sunlight streaming through the myriad glass panes above. It's so beautiful it's unearthly, like a theatrical setting for a fantastical dream, as if one of those perfectly proportioned, mysteriously lit, arched interiors in Renaissance paintings has suddenly blossomed into life. 'Oh so beautiful, Anatole,' I say. We stand there in the silence, him proudly smiling into the space as if to say, 'Look at this world I inhabit.'

Time for more instruction. We return downstairs, passing through muralled halls with showcases of mythical objects — Trojan pottery, jewelled reliquaries, fabulous bronze beasts.

In the entrance hall we arrive at a console table with a neat stack of large handsome books about the school and the museum's collections. Anatole buys one for me. He flicks through the introductory text, each page with a column of Russian and its English translation on the right, finds the pages he wants, and indicates that he must attend to business for a few minutes and that I'm to read this section while he's away. He holds my eye, conveying to me, 'I'm serious now; this is no joke,' and disappears.

'The wind was blowing snowdrifts in the formerly luxurious Museum halls,' I read. 'The masters of restoration would be needed to revive the beautiful city from the ruins and to cure its terrible wounds.' But there were no masters, no teachers; they had perished in the war or during the Siege of Leningrad, their tools along with them. 'We looked for those who were still alive as if we were in search of unique precious stones.'

Reading on, I learn of the central role of Anatole's school in what followed. In 1945 the Soviet of People's Commissars resolved that it would be reopened as a school for the architectural restoration of St Petersburg. Three masters were eventually located and restoration work commenced at the school itself, where the fifteen to seventeen year old girls and boys recruited as students — working under circumstances that were virtually impossible — learnt on the job: marble work, inlay, fretwork, mural painting, cabinet-making, metal chasery — it's endless. These were the humble beginnings of St Petersburg's masters of reconstruction. It took months for them just to clear the rubble. The school itself took nearly a decade to restore. Then work began on the palaces, work that continues into the new millennium.

By the time Anatole returns I am thoroughly chastened. Coming from a country where the horrors of war have never occurred, how could I possibly know the means by which the inhabitants of a magnificent city retain their sanity in the aftermath of its destruction? It's one thing to look at a reconstructed palace; it's quite another to begin to understand that this is what Anna Akhmatova, St Petersburg's Cassandra, foresaw: that after its martyrdom at the hands of Stalin and Hitler the city would one day be resurrected.

Garlands of fresh flowers have been placed at the bases of the elaborate wrought-iron lamps that flank the outside entrance. Anatole waits while I photograph them. I later learn from Ada that they are offerings, placed there by hopefuls who have applied to study at the school.

———•◦•———

Galina Petrovna Morkovin spent her working life as a translator for the Ministry of Culture, but this isn't why I've come to see her. She's the descendant of a member of pre-Revolutionary St Petersburg's intelligentsia. Her mother, who worked at the Hermitage in the twenties, was an aristocrat who came from a family of admirals that dates back to the eighteenth century.

Galina Petrovna, who I've been warned appreciates the use of her patronymic, lives in a street of decaying baroque residences near the Tauride Gardens. Her apartment building is decorated with fabulous classical statues that strut and gesture against the sky. A high box window juts from the second storey, supported by bare-breasted caryatids with swirling draperies and garlands of fruit.

Minutes later, to my delight, I'm sitting at one of these very windows on a decrepit Empire couch with two chinchilla cats, expressing astonishment at the richness of the surroundings I find myself in: the silverware and gilt frames, the Venetian mirrors and bronze sphinxes, the Aubusson carpet and the exotic Brussels tapestry with its panther and turbaned Negro. The tapestry is faded and the carpet threadbare, but still it's as if I've stepped back in time; it seems inconceivable that such an interior could exist here in private hands.

'This … wrecks is all we have left of a great house, my dolling,' says Galina Petrovna with a disdainful sweep of her ancient arm, the twitching chihuahua on the high arm of her chair ducking its head just in time. 'These poor bits of antiques, these bric-a-bracs that you call it, for decades my mother hid them away in a cousin's house in Omsk. My poor mother, she was a frightened woman. She knew how to keep quiet I can tell you, my dolling. And she taught me too. I spent my life keeping quiet.'

'But now you can speak,' nods the elderly gentleman across the table from us, her husband Alexei, whose sallow skin, eyes, hair and cardigan are of the same tonality.

'Now I can speak,' she repeats, voice raised. 'My mother thought if neighbours saw she had beautiful things, they'd denounce her, and she was right to think this because in Soviet times people would always denounce their neighbours. They do so because they want to look like good comrades, but also they are afraid. And the Soviets, they hate beauty. If you have something beautiful, immediately they suspect you. Deliberately, from the beginning, they destroy Russian culture. My mother see very strange things at the Hermitage that make her frightened. It's lucky she see this because at the time many people think Bolsheviks are okay and they trust them. But what

Left Siberian wolves at the Museum of Zoology

Below Lion at the Leningrad Zoopark

my mother see, she can't believe it but she knows not *ever* to trust them, not *ever* to say anything, to pretend *always* to be invisible, so she survive. This sounds as if she was weak and a coward, but no, she was very strong, very smart and in charge of her life, but under the Bolsheviks and later the Soviets it was not possible to be in charge of your life. Deliberately she pick a husband she think can protect her. My father, he was member of the Cheka. You know what is Cheka?'

'The secret police?'

'Yes. Under Stalin become KGB. But Lenin and Trotsky set it up as Cheka. And you know it is through my father and his friends that my mother finds answer to big mystery. I must tell you the whole story. She told me nothing till my father die and she is old woman. Then she told me everything and it was very hard for me to believe. Some of it was like she brought a shining dream into our grey world but most of it was like terrible nightmare. Of course now I know everything she told me was true. But let us eat. Alexei, if you make the tea we can begin the lunch.'

Her husband seems to be captivated by dust motes whirling in a sunbeam.

'Alexei,' she urges gently, leaning forward and stroking his hand, prompting him to turn to her with a startled look. She speaks soothingly to him in Russian and, with a little bow in my direction, he heads off through double doors with engraved glass panelling, a black and white borzoi trailing after him.

Galina Petrovna turns to me. 'He is philosopher, you know, and his mind is … elsewhere.'

Amused, I smile into her blue-grey eyes, youthful and alert in her lined face. She returns my smile and adjusts the antique comb in her French knot, her fine flyaway hair not yet entirely grey. She wears a dark red Italian-style knitted jacket with gold coin buttons; it's synthetic, cheap, like most Russian clothes, but on Galina Petrovna it's Armani.

'At first when my mother work at Hermitage — for nothing practically, just enough to buy scraps of food — everything is normal. Then many things start to disappearing, the best masterpieces. Suddenly some very special masterpiece by Rembrandt or Botticelli is not there on wall any more. Mama, my mother, can't believe her eyes so she ask Hermitage director and he say he's too busy to talk. And one day she sees a blank spot on the wall and she nearly scream out with agony because this is a painting she love so much, the most won-derful Tiepolo painting that was purchased by Catherine the Great herself, and she runs to the director, crying, and he says she must be quiet and secretly he tells her yes, they have been assigned but she must say nothing and he is doing what he can but she can see he is very upset and frightened.'

'What happened to these paintings?'

'You don't know?' she queries me with penetrating eyes.

'No. How would I know?'

'I thought maybe everybody know by now. But of course even in Russia many people don't know about this. Only in the last years my American visitors have told me things. So I must tell you whole story of what happens to some Hermitage paintings and Romanov imperial jewels and thousands of other treasures.

'Bolsheviks say all this things belong to Russian people so right at beginning in 1917 Lenin nationalise all palaces and collections and treasures. But let me tell you, my dolling, they don't nationalise it for the people, no. They do this to have a lot of wealth they do with what they like. They say is for industrialisation of Russia and, yes, some of it they use for this but who has ever seen the arithmetic for what happens to the rest? I ask you, my dolling. When my mother sees disappearing some best pictures in Hermitage by Raphael, Valesquez, Rembrandt, she doesn't know what happens to them but she sense in her deepest instincts already never to breathe this to anyone, even before Hermitage director say this to her. She tell me later, "I smell mysterious darkness, like some black ... abyss."

'She marry my father and have me and my brother and she say nothing. She maybe little bit happy because my father has contacts and their life is not so bad and later they move into this apartment, which used to be owned by Stroganoffs or Yusupovs or one of this princes, and it remind her of happy childhood.

'One day my father come home and tell her Stalin pass new decree. This is secret decree but he talk to my mother about it because he curious about something. He know my mother doesn't talk. He's smart my father and he know my mother hide things even from him. This is about 1928, I think. Stalin's decree say it's okay to sell Russia's treasures. All museums must assign best treasures and sixty percent will be sold overseas. My father know about this because is his job to check up on museums. Of course Mama's heart is beating because now she understand what will happen to Hermitage paintings. But even my father who is no particular friend of artistry is very curious about whereabouts of most wonderful Russian treasure. He say years ago Cheka seized this from Yusupov Palace where it was hidden. A giant pure silver statue of baptism of Russia, an antique that weighed tons. This was seized with collection of Fabergé eggs and solid gold dinner service and poof! Disappear. Nobody ever see this things again. My father think now maybe it reappear to be sold overseas. But no, this Russian treasure, *priceless*, is evaporated. What happened to things like this? I ask you.'

'What happened to the pictures from the Hermitage?' I ask.

'European dealers sell on international market. I have American friends come to see me who live in Washington and they tell me some of this pictures is in art museum there. They send me book of museum and one is on poster so I know this is true. One particular beautiful one, most special favourite of my mother, *Madonna Alba* by Raphael.'

'This was from the Hermitage collection?' I say, surprised.

'Yes, my dolling. I tell you. And maybe twenty, thirty other masterpieces in this Washington museum are from Hermitage.'

'But how ... ?'

'Listen, my dolling, these picture come on international market in 1930s and who owns them is maybe not specified. They just appear from nowhere. Art dealer doesn't announce, "This is from Hermitage." Stalin, he's mad, but not crazy. Maybe some scholars in these international museums, they know is from Hermitage. Who knows? Who remembers now? Selling this pictures is crime against Russia and crime against Russian people, but museums in Europe, America, buying them is not committing crime. They come onto market legally.'

She narrows her eyes and looks at me wickedly. 'You know, before I mention you this Tiepolo painting?'

'The one Catherine the Great purchased?'

'Yes, because this subject suit Catherine's personality so much. Almost like Tiepolo paint this picture for Catherine. You know what is subject of this picture, my dolling?'

'No, what was it?'

'I think maybe you know this picture. This is why I especially mention it you. My American friend tell me she see this picture in Australia.'

'The only Tiepolo I know of in Australia is ... *The Banquet of Cleopatra*.'

'Yes!' Galina Petrovna takes my hand in both of hers and presses it excitedly. 'Tell me what it look like.'

'It shows Cleopatra dropping the pearl into the wine, showing off to Caesar. It's said to be Tiepolo's masterpiece. And Cleopatra's dressed not as an Egyptian but in eighteenth century style, similar perhaps to the way Catherine dressed. And you're right, Galina Petrovna. I remember now. This painting is in Melbourne, which is where I live, and I think it says on the label that the painting was acquired from the Hermitage.'

'So you tell me this must be the one?'

'Yes, I'm sure.'

'I can't tell you, my dolling, how I would love to see this picture, not just for my curiosity but for my mother.'

'I'll send you a poster of it.'

'You promise me?'

'I promise.'

Alexei emerges through the door carrying plates piled with chicken and frankfurts. Galina Petrovna excitedly tells him about the poster. He nods benignly at me and returns to the kitchen, the borzoi shadowing his every step. He re-emerges with a bowl of steaming potatoes and a tinned orange cake.

We eat from plates decorated with peacocks, from the famous St Petersburg porcelain factory.

Alexei places saucers of chicken under the chinchillas' noses and feeds bones to the dogs, who politely wait their turn.

Galina Petrovna goes on talking and making broad gestures with her arms between mouthfuls of food and sips of tea. Just as her mother had to keep silent, Galina Petrovna loves to talk. And as she goes on speaking it strikes me that I am hearing another heartbreaking narrative of loss; St Petersburg's lost palaces, lost masterpieces, lost priceless treasures.

And now I hear of its lost inhabitants.

'My mother was a haunted woman. She couldn't speak but her memories wouldn't go away. To tell me the truth when I was younger was to put me in danger. It was safer for me not to know. She deliberately brought me up to be ordinary, just like everyone else — to blend into the picture and not stand out because to stand out was to have their evil eye on you, and then you were finished. Her sister stood out, her clever sister Varvara, my aunt. She was exceptional young poet who read with Mayakovsky in the 1920s at the poetry readings.'

'You know what Mayakovsky said?' asks Alexei unexpectedly.

'No,' I say.

'That Russia was the only place in the world that took poetry seriously, so seriously that they murdered their poets. They murdered Mayakovsky two years after he said this.'

'And Varvara,' chimes in Galina Petrovna, 'she was sent to a labour camp. She died before I was born. Thousands of clever young Petersburg people like Varvara at first believe so strongly in Revolution and Bolshevik slogans. Peace, land and classless society, this was the promise and this is what they all believe in and what they think is going to happen after Revolution. When it doesn't, they protest loud and make their voices heard and they are quickly silenced.

'So Varvara and her passions and beliefs was a second lesson for my mother in keeping quiet and fading into the background. You know at the end of her life my mother used to say that St Petersburg intelligentsia brought about its own destruction because it was in love with Revolution as if it was some romantic idea. These were Russia's most brilliant people, the best educated and most cultivated.'

'The people you see around you now are not St Petersburg people,' says Alexei. 'They came here from the regions to find food and work during the Second World War. Many came from parts of Siberia.'

'What happened to the St Petersburg people?' I ask.

'Some were killed in the civil war after the Revolution. Some of the intelligentsia — thousands of artists, writers, thinkers and art collectors — were deported or escaped to Europe or America, but most of them were murdered or sent to Kazakhstan or other camps in the thirties. As soon as Stalin arranged for his one-time friend, General Kirov, to be murdered, this seemed to set off something in his brain. A popular little rhyme of the time went: *Oh, things got even horrider,/ Stalin got Kirov in the corridor.*

'But things got much more horrible, much more, to a point where it was beyond people to believe what was going on under their noses. The purges began, and the Great Terror took hold. The members of the cultural elite that managed by some miracle to survive those years died of starvation during the Siege of Leningrad.'

Alexei sighs deeply and rests his head in his hand. Galina Petrovna opens her mouth to speak but gently he silences her.

Frowning at the tablecloth, he says, 'I often ask myself if St

Petersburg still exists. I say to myself, what is a city? Is a city a place and its buildings, or is a city its people? If the life of a city is its people, and its buildings and bridges the empty stage where people enact their lives, then St Petersburg no longer exists. And it's a very strange thing.' He looks up at me. 'Before the Revolution, writers like Gogol and Biely were already writing about St Petersburg as a city of ghosts and illusions. As if they sensed the end was near.'

'We've lived through strange times,' says Galina Petrovna. 'When you don't know any different you think this is what life is. In those days we thought we were happy.'

'We thought we were happy,' echoes Alexei.

———•◦•———

I'm visiting Tamara with Ada and Mitri, and Tamara's black and white TV set is on. Tamara seems distracted tonight, doubtless because of the situation with her apartment. She's always found a diversion in television, which is still a novelty here, but now it's on most of the day and all through her insomniac nights.

Images of Russia's last Tsar, Nicholas II, and the Romanov family come onto the screen. These are followed by an old woman wearing a terrible nylon wig the same smoky tonality as the cat she's cradling. She spouts forth authoritatively for the cameras. More Romanov images, and then other Russians take turns at speaking into the interviewer's mike.

Tamara scoffs.

'What's going on?' I ask.

'The Russian Orthodox Church want to make Tsar Nicholas a saint. They ask many people what they think of this,' she explains.

'A saint,' I repeat, flabbergasted. 'Why do they want to make him a saint?'

'Because he achieve a lot,' says Tamara, deadpan, disdainful.

'What did he achieve?' I ask.

'The Revolution,' quips Ada.

We laugh uproariously. My friends' reverence for the Romanovs does not extend to the last of them. This doesn't seem to be the case with the rest of Russia.

'What do people think of this?' I ask Tamara. 'What was that old woman with the cat saying?'

'This woman talk about icon of Tsar Nicholas as saint that was taken around Russia this year and people say it produce miracles. She say she see this icon and beautiful mysterious perfume come from it and when she pray to it her heartache go away. She confesses her sin of being Communist and afterwards this icon appear to her in a dream.'

'And others say Nicholas and his family should be saints because they suffer so much,' says Mitri, who seems to find food for thought in this.

'Sh,' says Ada. An elderly woman appears on the screen with tears streaming down her face, wringing her hands.

'This woman say she was desperate to get from Dnepropetrovsk to Kiev but she had no money,' says Ada. 'But she see icon of Tsar and a miracle happen. A stranger came up to her and gave her the two *hryvnas* for the ticket.'

We're silent, eyes glued to the screen.

In less than a week, the *St Petersburg Times* headline announces, ROMANOV FAMILY GIVEN SAINTHOOD.

I read that after eight years of debate which threatened to split the Russian Orthodox Church, Tsar Nicholas II, along with his wife and five children, have been canonised due to their 'widespread popular veneration'. Over the past three years, the Church claims, proof of their sanctity has been received in the form of the many miracles which have been documented.

'Finally we have lived to see people start to revere our Father Tsar,' Maria from Kiev, who declined to give her second name, is quoted as saying.

The Chair of the Moscow Patriarchate's Commission agrees that Nicholas did not deserve sainthood for the way he ruled the Russian state and the Church. 'But both he and his family deserve sainthood as passion bearers for their pious life and humble death in Bolshevik captivity.'

The Russian Orthodox Church wishes to emphasise that the canonisation of the last Tsar and his family is by no means a canonisation of monarchy as a form of government.

So the overwhelming sense of loss felt by my friends and others I encounter is not, as I'd presumed, confined to St Petersburg. All of Russia, it seems, longs to return to the past and recover not only lost palaces, masterpieces and brilliant artists and thinkers, but institutions and concepts as well, ones that are centuries old.

The longer I remain in St Petersburg, the more I understand how deeply entrenched is this grieving over the past, this hankering for it. The obsession with what has been lost is so powerful that it has taken on a life of its own, an impetus, which has now reached a climax in the sanctification of the last of the tsars. Lenin must be turning in his grave.

NETHERWORLD

At the Hermitage end of Nevsky Prospekt, near the Moika Canal, is a delectable three-storey shop of pre-Soviet glamour. It specialises in items of feminine fetishism: perfume, shoes and handbags. The shop's among a feast of art nouveau buildings whose beauty Salvador Dali described as 'edible'. Pavlova shopped here surely, and probably Akhmatova as well. Items of such quality are rarely found in St Petersburg and here in my favourite shop they are enthrallingly low-priced.

I mount the staircase that winds around the sprouting iron lift-cage, enjoying its sinuous floral forms as I spiral upwards. I reach the first floor and pause at a spectacle of handbags. I adore being here: it's the soft amber-lit ambience of Belle Époque feminine luxury. Green leather boots with pointy toes demand my attention and I stroll through the broad inviting doorway of the shoe shop on the left.

Russian boots. Always, since as a small child seeing Greta Garbo play Anna Karenina, I've wanted a pair of classic

Russian boots — fur-lined and creasing into soft folds at the ankle.

Now my stockinged leg slides into the soft thick lambskin interior of one of a pair in the softest taupe leather. They're not classic, but who cares; they're comfortable, have buckles at the ankles, reach midway up my long thighs and cost around twenty Aussie dollars. I can't believe I've found something so much more than perfect and raise my short skirt a little to admire the generous fur turnover at the top. I discover when I pull this up that the boots reach nearly to my crotch. So I can wear the boots either super-high or generously fur-cuffed. Is there no end to their virtues?

I slide into the other one and turn with my back to the long mirror, swivelling my head to appraise the back view.

Cuffs pulled up. Cuffs rolled down, exposing the fleshy tops of my slender thighs. I hitch my skirt higher, turn around to face the mirror again and step back to admire the overall effect. They're my dream boots and I'm besotted.

Behind me, in the mirror, is the reflection of a man standing in the doorway. He's been watching me.

I return to the seat, feeling his eyes on me. Such an openly admiring, lustful look. I'm repelled by men in uniform and this one — fortyish, well built, snake's eyes — is dressed in the rough khaki of a Russian army officer, authoritative cap and all. As I unzip my bag he has the nerve to look me up and down appraisingly, so I point my face in his direction, open my eyes wide and look long at the bridge of his nose. This has the effect of making me cross-eyed and demented looking and always puts men off.

Not the Russian soldier. He smiles conspiratorially.

I'm not prepared to treat him to the spectacle of my removing the boots, so I leave them on, pay for them smiling wordlessly at the salesgirl and exit the shop, brushing past him rudely.

As I reach the stairs I look back. Why, why do I do this? My obsession with looking drives my life.

At the entrance to Nevsky Prospekt metro I stop, as usual, to admire the Persians offered for sale by the women who gather there daily. The silky kittens sit calmly in the women's arms. I sense the soldier near me even before I see him throw some coins into the tin held by the girl with the performing dogs. I walk on, perversely gratified that he's following me but a little annoyed. What does he think I'm going to do, for god's sake? Lead him to some dark doorway, some dim room, where he can run his hands over me?

But that's a fantasy of mine, isn't it? To be in a foreign city, lock gazes with a handsome stranger, and lure him inside the dark entrance of a deserted building where I lean languorously against a wall, lift my skirt and close my eyes, smilingly waiting for the first pleasurable shock of his body against mine. No words are exchanged; the fantasy is always enacted in silence. Sometimes the stranger isn't handsome; he's ugly or brutish, which gives a jagged edge to the excitement.

The scenario now is ripe for this kind of possibility. I have an hour to kill. I look over my shoulder; yes, he's still behind me. The soldier isn't ugly, not by any means, but it's his uniform that's the frisson factor in this attraction–repulsion scenario. In any case, I think as I pass under Yeliseevsky's canvas awnings, he's a *Russian* soldier. Old footage of beautiful dead young men half buried in the snow flashes into my mind; in history's bank of images, Russian soldiers are the victims of war, not the agents of it.

Three blocks later as I turn left at the Anichkovsky Bridge with its rearing bronze horses, I look back for the fifth or sixth time and, yes, he's still a few metres behind me, and for the fifth or sixth time I laugh and he smiles broadly. By now it's become a game. I feel detached from the situation, my mind floating in a world of possibility. This carries such a sense of freedom that I momentarily feel utterly happy.

As I walk beside the Fontanka Canal, I wonder if I'm unconsciously heading this way because beside the baroque Fountain House and its garden of dry weeds is a forest of tall trees with shady undergrowth. I picture myself leaning against one of those trees and smiling, eyes closed. I reach the fence and photograph its wonderful lion gate.

Beyond the little forest is the silent apartment of Anna Akhmatova, who saw her fate as intertwined with St Petersburg's, choosing to remain in the city, rather than flee to

Europe, and bear witness to its doom and destruction. Since her death it's been a museum to her, which I visited yesterday. Incredibly, its two gentle babushkas don't treat the presence of visitors as a personal affront. They told me that trusted friends who came here long ago when their adored poet was still alive — one of them spoke some English while the other nodded solemnly — were secretly obliged to commit Akhmatova's latest verses to memory as she knew anything she wrote down would be used against her or those she loved.

I look at my watch. It's later than I think — impossible now to waste time entering through the gate, leaving it ajar and walking into the shadowy deserted garden as I was daring myself to do. If I'm to allow myself sufficient time to twice change trains and locate the connecting platforms between Mayakovskaya and Vitebsk stations in the labyrinthine underworld of the St Petersburg metro system, I must head back to Nevsky Prospekt now. Ada and Tamara will be waiting for me at Vitebsk at 1 p.m. and already it's 12.05.

Abruptly I about-face, knowing this will confuse my follower but unwilling to think up quick ways to evade him; to admit him into my plans for the day now is to place him too solidly in reality. He will remain a fantasy figure and must soon disappear as abruptly as his reflection appeared in the mirror.

He's hesitating and stops and waits as I walk quickly in his direction. He looks surprised, excited, a little alarmed. I'm almost level with him and he can see I'm going to stride straight past him so he steps smilingly in my path, whispers something I don't catch. What clever snake's eyes he has, what cheekbones and white even teeth. I fix my eyes on his odious officer's cap, pronounce, 'I'm in a hurry and don't understand Russian,' and keep walking, not before registering his pleasure at discovering I'm a foreigner. It strikes me that he doesn't look like a soldier at all, more like an actor playing a soldier.

I turn into Nevsky, cross Sadovaya, and enter the grandiose cream and gold interior of Mayakovskaya metro station with its neoclassical statues, my mind focused on the difficult negotiations ahead, half aware of the soldier's presence behind me. I'm determined to conquer my fear of St Petersburg's cavernous metro system, with its bewildering connections in claustrophobic mazes hundreds of metres under the earth.

I stand in a long fast-moving queue memorising the Russian for 'two tokens please' and the purchase takes place so smoothly I feel a small sense of triumph as I drop one of them in a slot and pass through one of fifteen or so creaking turnstiles. So as not to be swept up in the impetus of the rushing crowd I stand to one side against a wall and study my metro map, where the stations are translated in English above their Russian names in Cyrillic script. This is what really terrifies me, the fact that once I get down there I'm robbed of the power to communicate. I can't read the signs and nobody understands what I'm saying — it's literally a nightmare experience. And how like a nightmare these stations are, subterranean caves of hallucinatory beauty where a Hades might entice a Persephone.

On my map Ada has pencilled directions next to some of the stations — take escalator, turn left, turn right, take second escalator down, turn left, take train at this platform, left side, and so on. I take a deep breath and plunge into the crowd to follow her instructions. The dark mahogany escalators spew out their metal steps at a furious pace, processing commuters like cogs on a conveyor belt, but today I forbid myself to hesitate too long before I step on and with hundreds of others plunge deep down into the earth at rocket speed. A suffocatingly hot wind fans my hair up and out behind me, blasting an acrid smell of ancient dust full in my face. Last week I calculated with Tamara that each escalator can plunge a hundred metres; after making the left and right turns as per Ada's instructions, the thought of facing a further plunge in the second escalator makes my chest tight but I plunge on. I try not to think of what Tamara said, that St Petersburg's metro system is unusually deep because of the levels of swampy substrata that had to be dug through before hitting bedrock, that it's so deep it goes under the Neva. The mental picture of myself as a human ant moving through a vast network of Stygian tunnels beneath all that wateriness makes my head swim, and leads inevitably to thoughts of entrapment. God, it stinks down here in this foul brown air.

I find the right platform, a train arrives in less than a minute, as they always do, and I board it anticipating the relief I'll feel in a few minutes. I find a seat and stare at Russian faces, tired and grey in the harsh light. A blonde teenager's is extraordinarily beautiful but most are far less cared for than Australian ones: bad skin, bad teeth and dull hair, but more human somehow, vulnerable, more loveable.

At the next stop I emerge at Dostoevskaya, a seedy art-deco tango hall of a station, all pastel stucco work and ambient yellow side lighting. This time I've memorised Ada's instructions and I almost take pleasure at being caught up in the dynamism of the crowd, walking and making turns and riding escalators in the same rhythm and direction as the thousands of Russians I'm surrounded by. It's like being an extra in an Eisenstein film. Another platform, another tango hall, but this side of the station is no longer Dostoevskaya, it's Vladimirskaya. This is one of the confusions of St Petersburg's metro system for visitors: several of the larger stations have two names and two adjacent sections with separate entrances.

The worst is over, I think. The train that will deliver me to Vitebsk thunders into the platform and I board it, surprised to find it packed sardine tight. So many people crowd in I find myself being pushed toward the back of the carriage and have to strain and jostle to stay reasonably near the door so I'll be able to get out when we reach Vitebsk, only two stations away. I turn my body around to face the door and above a short fat woman in front of me is the face of the Russian soldier. I gape, not knowing what surprises me most, the fact that he's here now or the fact that he'd slipped my mind.

It's hard not to smile so I roll my eyes heavenwards as I do. This makes him laugh and with one deft manoeuvre and an apology to the short woman, he's standing right in front of me, so close I notice his cheek flush slightly.

I really don't know what to say — what's the point anyway; he won't understand me. The train takes off and to the accompaniment of its screeches and lurches he speaks words I don't understand, but the rhythms alone are seductive, the tone and smoky quality of his voice. He's standing lopsidedly and I become aware that the back of his hand is resting casually against the fur cuff of my boot. He begins running his fingers lightly and caressingly over the fur, closing his eyes and tilting his head back, and I can see he's been dying to do this. I move close against him and breathe in his prickly wool smell. The train lurches and he puts his other arm around my waist to steady me. I stand pressed against him, rocking with the rhythm of the train, feeling the heady warmth of his breath and shaven cheek against mine. The train's approaching Pushkinskaya Station and I'm fighting a desperate desire to bite his neck by picturing Ada's and Tamara's faces when I arrive accompanied by a soldier with his hand up my skirt. How *am* I going to deal with this when we alight at Vitebsk? The train shrieks to a stop, the doors fly open, and I crane my neck so I can see past his head through the window as passengers near the door alight. Suddenly I'm with them, pushing determinedly against boarding passengers. This is not Pushkinskaya Station. I know the soft cream décor of palatial Pushkinskaya, one of numerous tributes to Russia's eternally favourite poet, and this isn't it. I've been propelled through the wrong tunnel on the wrong train, whose doors now snap shut before my soldier can get out. I shrug in helpless confusion and blow him a kiss. He smiles ruefully as his face flashes past me. I stand there, dazed, staring at the tracks long after the train has disappeared.

Minutes later I'm experiencing an eerie sense of unreality as my eyes move from the fading Cyrillic script of the station sign to my metro map, scanning it for the matching letters. After repeated readings of the routes around Dostoevskaya, then the entire map, I have to face the grim fact that the name of this station is not on any route; I have no way of knowing where I am. Indeed, according to my map, where I am doesn't exist. The crowd has disappeared through the distant exits at both ends of the platform and I stand bereft.

Now two inrushing streams of people converge on the adjacent platform. How rhythmic the tides of movement are, like a futurist painting. I, too, walk the few paces to the platform, calculating that the way out of this maze is to board the train going back the other way; in the unlikely event that it doesn't return to Dostoevskaya, it will at least go back to a station whose name I can identify.

The train rumbles into the station, travelling, against all reason, in the same direction as the one I just alighted from. To board it is to go further into nightmare territory. I back away, stumbling against the trolley of a legless man as he propels himself through the nether regions of the crowd toward gaping train doors.

I stand on the deserted platform in the greenish gloom. Enormous neon chandeliers hang above me like giant weights. A heavy black cloud drifts into my consciousness and settles there: the image of myself so far beneath the city, so deep down in the earth. It's the unreality of it that's so disturbing; it's my first experience of the kind of St Petersburg Gogol wrote about, not just the absurdist one where a nose might take off from a general's face and begin to live a life of its own, but the ghostly gas-lit world of illusions where characters walk uncertain streets, pursued by their doppelgängers. I head for the distant exit, the one to the right, superstitious about the one *a sinistra*.

I mount a flight of stairs, traverse a tunnel, and find myself in a kind of low-ceilinged Romanesque crypt, all elephantine columns and dimness, lit, incongruously, by elaborate crystal chandeliers. Radiating from this hub are six or so staircases and passageways with signs above them. Of course I can't read the signs. Then it hits me. In a nightmare such as this the names of individual stations don't really matter, nor in the long run do directions for making connections; what really matters is the word for the most important signifier of all: EXIT. For this is, of course, the word that indicates the way out of the trap, the sign that denotes escape. All I needed to have done was to have written down the Russian for this in Cyrillic script and I'd be on my way out of here. For I've given up on the day, have renounced the weekend at the beach on the Gulf of Finland with Ada and Tamara that I was so looking forward to. All I want is to find my way out of the labyrinth.

I look around at the six signs, trying to work out if any of them look as if they might mean exit, or if there are two words the same on opposite sides of the space, which might denote the north and south or east and west exit signs found in many subways. No luck. I remember that my guide-book has a glossary and quickly retrieve it from my bag and, squinting myopically in the gloom, scan columns for the magic word 'exit'. All I find is 'entrance'. Thank you Lonely Planet.

I lean against one of the thick columns in the chandelier-lit blackness with thousands of faceless Russians milling around me and feel my throat constrict. The brown air smells metallic and it's stifling. I'm sweating in these boots. I close my eyes and dark undulating waves come at me out of the blackness. I picture letting go, sinking down and falling prone, passing over into unconsciousness, perhaps being trampled to death by these hundreds of feet. My chest's so tight I begin to hyperventilate and it's the terror of knowing that I could in fact hyperventilate until I suffocate that impels me to bring my mind back into control.

My left arm is tingling and alarmingly weightless but I focus on quickly, as surreptitiously as possibly, taking off the boots. Just the act of moving makes me breathless with panic so I tell myself I'll be able to breathe properly as soon as I get the boots off. It does bring relief, the sweat running down my back now feeling cool. The tightness is my chest has become heaviness, like a weight, and it hurts to breathe, but at least I'm breathing. I put my shoes on and look at my watch: 12.30. I stare at the dial in disbelief: I still have time to meet Ada and Tamara. The thought of the two of them standing at Vitebsk, probably for hours, on one of their rare Friday afternoons off, worried to death about what terrible calamity has befallen me, makes my fears, real as they are, seem like sheer neurotic indulgence. By the time I've quickly worked out a strategy I've forgotten to hyperventilate, even though the thought of negotiating what might be the entire six of those tunnels and stairways — two of which, I've noted, plunge downwards — fills me with terror. I head for an up staircase in dread of the entrapment that lurks beyond.

It's a chandeliered limbo of gargantuan proportions, a Gormenghast of ascending escalators. At the sight of such expansiveness the constriction in my throat and chest eases, the oppressive black cloud evaporates. This can only be the way out, the exit I sought moments ago which now, ironically, is not what I'm after. I allow myself a moment's fantasy of boarding one of those tall escalators and escaping out into the sunlight beyond, before I turn around and with a heart like lead go back down the steps, for the other station platforms, I am now forced to concede, will not be on the higher levels of the maze but down in the sinister depths.

Passing again through the crypt and willing myself to be mindless, I take one of the dreaded down staircases which, after some excruciatingly bewildering tunnels and twists and turns, leads, as I feared it might, to a descending escalator. I step onto its grinding metal teeth and plummet into the underworld, the hot wind flapping in my face like the wings of an evil bird.

Head spinning, I will myself to keep track of the direction I'm heading in. I board a train that is probably, I calculate, heading in the general direction of Vitebsk.

'*Pazhalsta*, Vitebsk?' I gasp at the young woman next to me as I sit down, amazed that I can still speak.

'*Nyet*,' she responds uncertainly, prompting the bearded man opposite to insist, '*Da, da.*'

Oh god, can't anything be straightforward? I shrug and produce my metro map, holding it out to the man. He manages to convey to me that I should get out at the next station, which is walking distance from Vitebsk. I study the map and see that from Dostoevskaya I've travelled in a triangle and that the phantom station I've just escaped from is in fact Sennaya Ploshchad. Strangely, its Russian letters are nothing like the ones I tried to match on the platform, which in any case was one word, not two. How can this be?

Seconds later I'm amidst a crowd ascending stairs, escalators, stairs, up, up into St Petersburg's streets and daylight's brightness. I emerge like a newborn butterfly from Tekhnologichesky Institut Station. A few trestle tables are lined up where women are selling vegetables and I pause in front of a pile of marrows, stupidly transfixed by their pale green forms. This must be relief, I tell myself, feeling only a numb awareness of my return to normality. The gloom below is still in my head; the soldier's face flashes by and I experience a pang of loss. Damn. Flattered by my intense interest in her produce, one of the women, chattering away, smilingly holds up the largest marrow for me to admire. I buy it. Moving on, I pause to put the marrow in the bag with the boots and look around me. There, across the road in clear view, are the tall stained-glass windows of Vitebsk, another superb example of St Petersburg art nouveau. I look at my watch: 12.58.

In the main hall Ada stands by the ticket window looking her wonderfully haughty self. As I approach I see she is actually looking very annoyed.

'Tamara is a very serious woman but she is always late,' she greets me.

'But it's only just one o'clock.'

'No. She must to meet me here fifteen minutes ago to get the tickets.'

'She'll be here soon. Ada, you must explain something to me. The other day I got off at a station that had a name different to the one on my map.' (I avoid telling her it's just happened, that I'd muddled her meticulous instructions.)

'Maybe is old Soviet name.'

'What do you mean?'

'Everything has the two names. When St Petersburg become Leningrad after Revolution, all the streets change as well. They are named after Lenin and Bolsheviks and so on. Nevsky Prospekt for example refer to Decembrist uprising and is called by crazy name of Prospekt October 15.'

'Stations too?'

'Yes. Everything. So when Leningrad change back to St Petersburg in 1991, everything change back to historical name. They replace all the signs but sometimes they forget.'

'So the station I'm talking about still had its old Soviet name.'

'Maybe,' she says, looking at me closely. 'Maybe you have Soviet experience at this station?'

'Very Soviet experience,' I say, thinking of its greenish gloom and Gogol and his ghostly doppelgängers. Perhaps St Petersburg, too, is haunted by a ghostly double, that of its Soviet past.

'You must tell me what happened. What has happened to you?' she almost shouts.

I smile and whisper, 'Well Ada, I was in this shop and I bought these boots.' I lift them out of their bag and show her. Stroking their soft lambskin cuffs she tells me they're beautiful but impractical, not snow proof. 'Then,' I continue, 'I lifted up my skirt and showed my panties to a soldier and he followed me all the way to the Fontanka ...'

'No,' she gasps, appalled.

'Here's Tamara,' I say, catching sight of the familiar figure almost running toward us, bulging bags in each hand.

'You must tell me this story after,' Ada whispers with, to my amazement, a gleam in her eye which tells me she secretly finds it titillating.

After the usual whispering, meaningful looks and negotiations — they always make me pretend I'm Russian so I don't have to pay an 'American' price — it's like passing some kind of test — we purchase the train tickets. We buy more food to take with us from the stalls at the station entrance and still have half an hour to kill. They take me on a tour of Vitebsk's elegant interiors, which are, thankfully, all above ground.

We peek inside at the alluring decor and the intimate seating and lighting of its grand but deserted restaurant, little changed since it opened in 1903. Its starched waiters, arrested in time, do nothing but stand and wait.

In comparison with the grinding proletarian world of the metro system, it's clear Vitebsk belongs to an earlier era of rail travel, an innocent Edwardian world — bourgeois, I suppose — of picnics in the country and weekend trips to the seaside.

Which is exactly what we are doing, now, in Russia, in the very city that gave birth to the Revolution nearly a century ago.

Aspects of St Petersburg often strike me like this, that in spite of it having staged what is probably the most massive social upheaval in the history of the modern world, some things here, remnants of once grand things, haven't changed since the twilight years of the Belle Époque.

NEW WORLD

———◆•◆———

The iron-red train filled with weekending St Petersburgers rattles north through flat woodland. This is how life everywhere must have been before the car, families travelling by train and then walking to their beach shacks. Clusters of passengers in the large carriage open parcels of food and there is that feeling, mildly exhilarating, of everyone sharing a holiday experience, all of us off for a sea spell.

A skinny, pinch-faced boy of about twelve enters our carriage and, standing in the aisle, embarks on a monologue. His expression is earnest and his tone a flat singsong, as if he's said it all a thousand times before.

'What's he saying?' I ask.

'He sell the toothpaste,' says Ada.

The boy moves through our carriage and into the next one, proffering a cylinder containing a few tubes as he goes, monotonously keeping up the sales pitch.

I look at Tamara sitting opposite me. She's wearing a

green checked cotton jacket and it suits her dark russet colouring. Her warm brown eyes are alert, but they're ringed with tiredness. She must plough through every busy day in a state approaching exhaustion, but she's grown used to it and it has become her normality.

'Have you looked at any more apartments?' I venture. It's at least a week since I've asked.

She frowns. 'They show me one but not in the centre.'

'Where? Is it a tenement?' I ask.

'No, is old apartment but *whfff*,' she flaps her hands in front of her face as if she's warding off evil, 'too dark. Is in Smolny region.'

'Near the Smolny Institute?' I ask, referring to the aristocratic girls' school from whence Trotsky and Lenin directed the October Revolution. 'I thought that was a good district.'

'No. Far from Institute, on other side of Tauride Gardens.'

Ada interjects and I stare out of the window as they converse heatedly in Russian, Tamara's tone becoming increasingly determined.

———•·•———

Strolling three abreast under a clear cerulean sky along a dusty country road with tall birches and wooden dachas, we pass makeshift stalls with baskets of red currants and potatoes for sale. We veer right at the beach track for a swim before making our way through the wood to Tamara's parents' dacha. Tamara comes here every weekend to bring them food.

Sinuous pine trees with clouds of foliage fringe the broad beach with its soft beige sand. The sea glints sapphire blue, an island off in the distance. The only blot on the landscape is the unspeakable public toilets, open cubicles with foully be-smirched tiles surrounding a hole in the ground; but I refuse to even consider such horrors on this sunny afternoon.

Tamara puts on her swimsuit in one of the gaily coloured, figure-five-shaped change cubicles. She emerges, a mermaid in an apple-green two-piece, plunges into the ocean and swims happily, strongly, until she's a distant blur. In spite of the sunshine, it seems to me too far north for swimming; this, for god's sake, is the Gulf of Finland.

Ada and I grow drowsy under the pines, watching the shadows of figures on the beach lengthen.

'That water must be freezing,' I say.

'Tamara is very strong woman,' replies Ada. 'Too strong maybe. I think she should take this apartment in Smolny but she won't permit me to persuade her.'

'She's very proud,' I say. 'She hates anyone telling her what to do and I can understand that.' I find some apples in one of the bags of food and hand one to Ada. 'I can't talk with Tamara like I can with you. I mean I feel as if I can talk to her about anything in the world except herself. I think she likes to keep it that way, and why not? But I'm so curious about her son's father. Do you know anything about him?'

'I never meet him but many people speak of him, not so

much now, but before. He was musician, very good composer and he is always in big trouble with Soviet authorities. He make the music with too much … dissonance and they refuse to allow it to be performed. This is not the Russian music they say, but anti-Russian political statement. Of course he is modernist composer. Is not necessary for me to explain to you because you understand situation with the art and is same crazy formalist problem with the music. He is very angry because his music is never performed so he begin to drink more and more.'

'What happened to him?'

'He die.'

'Of alcoholism?'

Ada shrugs. 'I think so, yes.'

'Thank god I never asked Tamara about him,' I say.

'But she leave him before he die, I think. Maybe he was very difficult and Tamara must think first of her son. You know, Stalin knew that vodka is terrible problem for Russian people and he try to outlaw it, but even he can't stop it.' She picks up a twig and jabs at the sand with it. 'But of course vodka is not such problem for Russian people, he himself is the big problem.'

I laugh and she looks sharply at me. Stalin is never funny.

We're silent for a while and then begin chatting about Mitri's parents, Vassily and Novimira, who worked on Russia's space program. I'm very excited about meeting them tomorrow, particularly Novimira — an early product of the

Soviet policy of equal education for women, she trained as a physicist in the 1940s.

Sunbaking women on this beach, as yet blissfully unfamiliar with western consumer ideals of feminine desirability, are unselfconscious about their thick, strong bodies. Even the frankly middle-aged and older ones wear two-piece costumes. Their absence of vanity makes them seem timeless, monumental like the bathers in Picasso's paintings.

I'm about to ask Ada how it is that Mitri, with such educated parents, missed out on an education, when Tamara emerges from the waves, mahogany hair streaming.

By the time we walk back around the curve of the shoreline fluffy clouds glow sunset orange. A yacht with red sails comes skimming toward us. I break into the chorus of 'Red Sails in the Sunset' and Tamara says excitedly, 'It is the same in popular Russian love story. The ship with the red sail is love. Look, it comes toward you.'

'No, it comes toward *you*.'

The beach track forks and we wave Ada farewell until tomorrow. At the edge of the wood we buy a big paper bag of perfect little potatoes.

———◦•◦———

Tamara's parents' tiny verdigris-blue dacha sits in a vegetal paradise in front of a forest of lindens and tall pines. The house has two magical features. It's positioned far off the main path and set sideways, facing the neighbours' attractive yellow house across a kitchen garden of beetroot, tomatoes and bright-leaved mineral lettuce. And above its second storey, in the high peak of the roof, is a mysterious attic window, eerily intriguing because there's no room up there, not even a door.

Tamara's parents come outside to welcome us, Ekaterina small and wiry with almond-shaped grey eyes and good bone structure like her daughter, and Ivanov gentlemanly, solidly built in spite of his one leg, his brown eyes hooded like Tamara's. Tragic eyes.

Immediately my heart goes out to them, so utterly benign, poverty-stricken and delighted to see us are they.

'*Ochen npiiatno*,' I say, having rehearsed this simple expression of pleasure at meeting them on the way here with Tamara.

Birdlike Ekaterina, beaming, claps her hands together and hugs me. She exudes vitality in spite of her penurious get-up: grey hair pulled back from her face with bobby pins, faded blue cotton dress and grubby sandshoes with no laces.

It seems even the poorest of educated St Petersburgers have access to a dacha during the summer. The couple occupy the downstairs only, living in one spartan room that contains two single beds, a table and a food preparation area like an alchemist's workshop, crowded with bulbous glass jars.

I wonder where we're all going to sleep tonight.

Tamara and I unpack the goodies we've brought from St Petersburg: two loaves of black rye, cheeses, a tinned ginger cake, cranberry vodka, chocolates, a very large marrow and provisions for the coming week.

After a meal of bread, salad and a delicious soup made of pickled vegies and fresh ones from the garden, they teach me how to play a card game called Fu. The logic of it escapes me, but with Ivanov's constant help I enjoy the game.

My inability to speak Russian — and, I confess, my lack of interest in learning it because I'm preoccupied, as always, with looking — makes me feel particularly awkward in circumstances like these. My neck aches and I keep rubbing it. I would love to converse directly with these loveable people.

We chat, nevertheless, as we play cards, Tamara translating.

Ekaterina senses my discomfort and constantly reassures me with smiling eyes, affectionately taking my hand every now and then and squeezing it. I'm a stranger from a distant land, so I must be made to feel comfortable, at home, loved. How gracious they are about my inability to communicate on a sophisticated level.

I learn that Ekaterina and Ivanov both trained as engineers. Ekaterina worked at the diamond mines in a remote part of Siberia, which is where Tamara was born and grew up. It's common for Russian women to work as engineers, they tell me, and was even fifty or sixty years ago, half a century before feminism opened the way for women to do so in the west.

'My mother wants particularly to tell you something,' says Tamara. 'She worked all her life as a metallurgical engineer. The Bolsheviks said that in the new society women and men would receive equal education and do equal work. And it's true, she say, that under Soviets she receive the same education as the men and did the same work. But she does not receive promotion like the men. She is very good at her job but after many years goes up only one small level.'

I tell them that sometimes it's still like that in the west too, and explain to Tamara the concept of the glass ceiling, which she in turn explains to Ekaterina. They're both intrigued by this idea of a transparent barrier preventing women reaching the top, and Ekaterina insists on learning how to say it in English. Ivanov, too, enjoys the term.

'Glass ceiling,' repeats Ekaterina, feeling the words, her head birdlike to one side.

I ask about Ivanov's leg and Tamara tells me he lost it when he was only nineteen, fighting the Germans in the Second World War. The two of them live hand to mouth on three small pensions, one of which is for this war injury.

Bedtime. The mattresses on the two narrow beds are rolled back and laid side by side on what spare floor space there is, leaving Ekaterina and Ivanov to sleep on the bases of their beds. Ekaterina insists that Tamara and I have the sheets; knowing she'll also insist I have her pillow, I pretend I don't use one. There are no curtains on the window and I'm trapped against the wall, unable to go to the toilet outside without waking up all the occupants of the room. I envisage a sleepless night, lying in the moonlight with an aching neck and full bladder, praying for the dawn. I look at my watch. It's only 9.30. God.

I lie there thinking Ekaterina and Ivanov are like characters in a morality tale; to lose a limb as a youth fighting in a terrible war; to be a metallurgical engineer when women in the west hadn't emerged from the kitchen; to be as intelligent and educated as they are, to go through the difficult times they have gone through and end up living an impoverished existence in old age, and — this is the crux of it — to retain purity of heart and be accepting of this and find such joy in the company of others ... I fall into a deep sleep and awake ten hours later.

It's Saturday morning and time for ablutions. As with most dachas, there's no plumbing here, no water or taps, but Russians have strange devices for everything. On the wall near the front door in the entrance, which doubles as a bathroom, is a metal container about a foot high which is filled from the top with water, obtained from a communal well. Having by now mastered the use of these, I push up the long knob at the bottom of the container; water trickles into a plastic bowl on a small table and I wash my face and hands.

After I roll up the beds with Tamara, Ekaterina forbids me to do anything else. I'm the guest. Ivanov says, 'When we come to Australia, you can wait on us.'

After a breakfast of tea, cheese and cake, I step into the verdant, deliciously moist-smelling natural world outside and sit on a plank propped up by some logs. I stare up at the surreal attic window, pondering its mystery.

Ivanov comes out and presents me with a gift, a wooden device with a rubber roller. Miming, he instructs me to rub the muscles of my back and neck with it for five minutes every morning. Tamara comes out and tells me if I do this the pain in my muscles will be gone within days.

'Why is he giving it to me?' I ask her.

'He say you rub your neck a lot. It must be causing you pain.' She tells me he made it himself and assures me he has another.

Tamara and Ekaterina lead me into the shadowy woods behind the dacha. We have two hours, Tamara informs me, eyes bright, to spend mushrooming and gathering raspberries before Ada arrives to take me to Mitri's dacha. Mushrooming is to Russian women as shopping is to American ones: an elation-inducing means of satisfying the female instinct for gathering.

Under a lacework of branches with leaves still dewy, we tread through damp undergrowth spongy with built-up mulch, slipping down creek banks, balancing across mossy logs over streams, trudging up gullies. We fan out. I lean against a thick pine trunk, inhaling the earth-pine smell, and watch the two of them disappear into the distance, Tamara in her yellow poloneck striding high along the top of a ridge, and Ekaterina, never taking her eyes off the ground for a second, half obscured by bracken. How these two women thrive on immersing themselves in the natural world; it makes their lives bearable. I look down and notice a tangle of vine darkly glistening with berries. 'Ekaterina!' I shriek excitedly.

'*La ochen rada poznakomitsia s vami*,' I say to Ekaterina and Ivanov, managing to memorise the entire sentence as Tamara nods her head at me like a schoolmistress. 'I'm so pleased to have met you.'

'*Udachi*,' they say, standing together outside the house, waving goodbye until Ada and I disappear from view. '*Udachi*.' Good fortune.

A brisk half-hour walk inland along a sandy, sun-dappled track and we reach a very old dacha, partly overgrown with vines, green paint peeling. As we pass through the creaking front gate we glimpse Mitri's parents, Vassily and Novimira, sitting at a table under boughs drooping with green apples. Kolbasa, a stray dachshund-cross hanger-on with silky black curls, sits next to them on the grass.

Vassily, a snowy-haired version of Mitri, rises eagerly to greet me, excitedly telling me in broken English how he loves the English, how 'so special' it is for him to meet an Australian, who are 'very near' to the English. Mitri has told him all about me and what a pity he's not here now. He must drive all the way from Moscow and will be here after lunch.

Novimira, more reserved, stands behind him but moves

forward to greet me, to my utter surprise saying in English, 'How lovely to meet you.'

'She learn this for you especially,' says Ada. 'She does not speak the English.' I must look mildly alarmed because Ada adds, 'You must not to worry. I am also very interested to learn about Novimira's work as the scientist, so it give me pleasure to translate her conversation with you.'

A lunch of tinned herrings, salads and little cakes is carefully laid out inside. The round table with its crisp cream tablecloth and gleaming glasses looks as if it, too, is paying the house a visit, for the kitchen-cum-verandah, like the rest of the dacha, is, shall we say, picturesquely tumbledown. Vassily steers me around missing floorboards as we make our way to the table. He fills our glasses with cranberry vodka and we raise them in a toast while he remains standing.

'To Winston Churchill,' he says unexpectedly.

'To Winston Churchill,' we chorus.

I choke on the vodka and they laugh because they think I've been fooled by its lolly-pink colour.

'Winston Churchill was a big, big man,' Vassily tells me. 'I love England very much.'

'Vassily lived through the Siege of Leningrad,' explains Ada.

'I owe my life to England,' he adds emotionally.

Novimira, a handsome woman with thick white curls, smiles at me quietly.

'Russians have very very hard life. They are used to this so they are strong,' says Vassily. 'But not even Russians can survive Siege of Leningrad and starvation. In the Second World War the English and American convoy saved Russia.'

'Vassily loves everything English, including its literature,' Novimira conveys to me.

'I like the English poet Burns,' he says, refilling our glasses.

English, Scots, to a Russian it's all the same.

'Novimira is such a beautiful name,' I say, wanting her to talk about herself. 'It's the first time I've heard it.'

'The male version, Novimir, is more common. But my parents wished me to have this name because they believed in the Revolution; they'd participated in it. Novimira means "new world" and they wanted me to be a citizen of this new world. My mother imagined that men and women would be equal in every way in this new world, so she encouraged me to be a physicist.'

It seems extraordinary to me that this gentle, grand-motherly woman worked as a physicist during the west's most unenlightened decade, the fifties.

'Why a physicist?' I ask.

'After my parents read Einstein's *Theory of Relativity* they imagined that physicists would unlock the secrets of the universe. And that this would happen during the twentieth century.'

'And did you unlock any secrets?'

'Not exactly. But I worked with a very interesting team of

people, under a brilliant man, but he was very difficult. We worked on practical aspects of human survival in outer space.'

'What did you do exactly?' I ask.

'Did you hear of Sputnik in Australia?' she asks.

'Of course. The Sputniks were very famous. My mother told me about them when I was a little girl. She turned it into a kind of fairytale about the dog and the moon.'

'Yes,' she laughs. 'But the dog didn't go to the moon.'

'No, but it's necessary in a fairytale. Did you actually work on the Sputniks?' I ask, enthralled.

'Yes. At first I worked on the propulsion system and then I worked with the dogs.'

'Jules Verne wrote a book about the moon,' says Vassily, refilling our glasses again, to protests from Ada and Novimira. 'What was the name of this book? *The Journey* …'

'I don't know, Vassily,' I say. 'I'll think about it and tell you later. Novimira is going to tell us about the Sputniks.'

'It is so long ago …' says Novimira.

'Oh please,' I beg. 'Just ten minutes. Five minutes if you like. What's a propulsion system?'

'In order for a rocket to go up so far beyond the earth, it is necessary for it to go at a speed that seemed impossible in those days. So, in the beginning we worked on making a special fuel and a nuclear system to propel the rocket. My job was to find out what kind of materials could withstand such velocity in a space capsule. We did all kinds of tests and this is when I met Vassily.'

'You worked as a technician, Vassily?' I ask him.

'Yes. It was terrible in those days,' says Vassily. 'I can't tell you how hard our job was. After the war Russia was in a bad, bad state. Such conditions we worked in! You wouldn't believe them. I was technician but we had no technology. We didn't have any proper materials, not even tables to work at. The roof of the plant leaked and it was freezing. We had to invent everything ourselves.'

'How did you come to work with the dogs?' I ask Novimira.

'At first I worked on the best materials to build the capsule from. Then they became interested in what kind of capsule allowed a living creature to survive at such speeds. I ended up working with my team on this aspect of things and we made tests with the dogs.'

'Was this work kept secret?'

'Of course,' she breathes. 'It was associated with weapons development. All the rocket and aircraft factories were secret.'

'A big, big, secret,' says Vassily, placing two fingers across his lips.

'At first we knew very little,' continues Novimira. 'We didn't even know the name of the head scientist running our space program. Then, just before Sputnik I went up, my comrades learnt it was Korolev. Do you know who Sergei Korolev is?'

'No.'

'Korolev was a big man,' says Vassily.

'He was the greatest Russian scientist of the space program,' says Novimira. 'Maybe he hasn't been heard of yet in the west. Even most Russians didn't know about him until after his death. Korolev was such an unbelievably determined man that he convinced the authorities to release him from a gulag after he'd been imprisoned there for only a year. This was very unusual. Most people died in such terrible places.'

'Why was he imprisoned in a gulag?' I ask.

Novimira shrugs. 'Disloyalty or something like this. Some invented charge. He was arrested during the Stalinist purges.'

'So Stalin persecuted scientists as well?'

'Stalin persecuted all intelligent people because he wished nobody to know more than he did. About anything. Perhaps he was afraid they'd trick him if they knew something he didn't. And Korolev did trick Stalin. Perhaps he was the only person ever to do so,' she laughs.

Vassily leans across to me. 'Have I told you I very love England?' he says.

'Yes Vassily. How did Korolev trick Stalin?' I ask Novimira.

'Korolev's big ambition was to build rockets for space travel,' she says. 'But Stalin wasn't interested in such romantic dreams. Stalin's big interest was military power, military defence. So Korolev convinced him that work on rockets was necessary in order to develop intercontinental ballistic missiles for military defence. You see?' she laughs. 'Korolev was brilliant.' Her eyes gleam; for a moment she looks years younger.

'And Stalin made things very easy for Korolev,' she continues. 'Although this is the last thing he would have wanted to do.' She laughs again. 'Stalin was so secretive he didn't tell anybody anything.'

'When Stalin died and Khrushchev came to power, Khrushchev knew nothing about what was going on with the rockets,' laughs Vassily, thumping the table with mirth, checking our still-full glasses and refilling his own.

'So Khrushchev didn't interfere with the development of Sputnik,' continues Novimira. 'I remember Korolev told us one day,' she lowers her voice confidentially, 'that he'd been to a politburo meeting with Khrushchev to report on his work. Khrushchev and these big Party chiefs found it impossible to believe that something with such a simple shape could even fly. "It looks like a giant cigar," one of them said about the Sputnik we were developing. Korolev took them to the launching pad to explain how it worked and they kept tapping it to see if it was strong enough.' She and Vassily both laugh.

'What was Korolev like?' I ask.

'Korolev was a big man,' says Vassily.

'Dynamic,' says Novimira. 'He was absolutely convinced of his mission to send human beings into outer space.'

'Tell me about Sputnik and the moon dog.'

'Not moon dog,' Novimira wags her finger at me. 'You mean Laika, who went up in Sputnik II.'

'Do you know Pushkin?' Vassily asks me.

'Only *Evgenii Onegin*,' I say.

'Do you know Pushkin is Russia's greatest poet?' he asks me with feeling.

'Yes.'

Vassily stands up and, placing one hand over his heart and gesturing toward the window with the other, embarks on an impassioned recital of what I assume are verses by Pushkin. I don't understand a word and long to burst out laughing at his pained expression and melodramatic gestures, but soon the sheer beauty of the language seduces me and I succumb to its music.

A car door slams.

'Maybe this is Mitri,' says Ada. Vassily, his face beaming, goes to the door. It bursts open and there indeed is Mitri, with Felix tucked in his jacket. He passes the kitten to Ada. Father and son hug affectionately. Mitri then comes over to his mother and kisses her cheek in a rather formal way that surprises me. It seems out of character for Mitri.

Kolbasa leaps in the air, enthusiastically sniffing at Felix. Felix takes a curious sniff back. Very gingerly, Ada lowers the kitten to the floor, keeping her eye on Kolbasa. Felix takes a little run at him, leaping in front of his face like a mad thing. The dog nuzzles him. Instant friends. Ada and I exchange looks of amazement. Mitri opens the door so they can run outside to play.

'Thank you Vassily,' I say. 'Your Pushkin was very beautiful.'

'I know the very, very spot where Pushkin was killed,' Vassily announces. 'Do you know he was shot in a duel?'

I nod.

'We can show you this spot,' says Mitri. 'We must take you there.'

'Yes, we must take you there,' says Vassily. 'It's near Peter the Great's little wooden hut.'

'We'll go there tomorrow,' says Mitri.

'You Russians are fantastic the way you love your poets,' I say. 'You're still reciting Pushkin after nearly two hundred years. It's amazing.'

'Mitri knows nearly all Lermontov's poetry by heart,' says Ada proudly.

'So does Ada,' laughs Mitri.

'What about twentieth century poets?' I ask.

They shrug, uninterested. Ada fusses, putting together a plate of food for Mitri. Vassily pours a glass of vodka for him and manages to refill mine before I can stop him as Ada and Novimira do. Standing, he raises his glass.

'To 1941,' he says.

'To 1941,' repeats Mitri with feeling.

Vassily turns to me. 'Do you understand I love England?' he asks a little slurrily.

'Yes,' I say, patting his cheek.

'I have snow on my head but spring in my heart,' he tells me.

While Mitri talks with his father, Novimira tells me about

Laika, the three year old stray from the streets of Moscow who, after a period of intensive training, became the first living creature to travel in space.

Laika was known in the west as Limonchik, or Little Lemon. On 4 November 1957, the day after she was blasted into space at 30,000 kph, the appealing face of the Siberian-husky-cross commanded the front page of every newspaper in the west. Nicknamed Muttnik by the American press, she and Sputnik II transformed international perceptions of Russia. This sudden, unexpected scientific accomplishment from *muzhik* Russia was regarded by western nations as both magnificent and terrifying. As Limonchik orbited the earth at the inconceivable rate of once every 102 minutes, America looked to Cape Canaveral and the space race began.

The term 'animal rights' had not been coined but animal cruelty prevention societies from London to Tokyo expressed their abhorrence at Russia's cruelty in imprisoning Limonchik in a tiny hermetically sealed container and immobilising her in a space suit. 'Everything has been done to make Sputnik's tiny passenger as comfortable as possible,' Moscow radio assured the world. 'However sorry we may feel for the little Husky, we must think about the tremendous contribution she is making to science.'

For four days the world waited with bated breath to see if Limonchik would be catapulted safely to back to earth, as Soviet scientists claimed she would be. But Sputnik II, Novi-mira tells me, was not designed for recovery. The batteries that operated Limonchik's life-support system ran down and the air in her capsule ran out. Life slipped away from Laika a few days into her journey.

'Most of the later ones lived,' Novimira reassures me. 'Linda, or was it Strelka, had six puppies a few months after her space flight. Khrushchev gave one of these to the American President Kennedy.'

'I first heard about Arfstraalia in Jules Verne's *The Children of Captain Grant*,' says Vassily. 'Do you know Jules Verne?' he asks me.

'Yes, but I haven't read that one. Nabokov liked it, I think. He mentions it somewhere.'

'Does he really?'

'Yes.'

'Do you know I love Nabokov?' he asks. Vassily thinks on this and becomes a little tearful. He must have drunk a quarter of a bottle of vodka by now. 'But Nabokov love only Nabokov.'

In the white house next door, Ada and I chat with Mitri's childhood friends. This is where the famous *banya*, an age-old Russian cleansing ritual, is to take place and I'm a little nervous. We sit under a gazebo, surrounded by a garden of tall gladioli, sunflowers and red chrysanthemums. Jerry, a handsome, pure black German shepherd, lies sprawled at my feet.

Mitri appears. 'It's ready,' he says, rubbing his hands gleefully.

Svetlana, a statuesque woman with the palest blonde cropped hair and luminous white skin, leads us through rows of sunflowers to a pine houselet at the bottom of the garden. In the small change room she shows me a lethal-looking faggot she's prepared: birch branches still wearing their leaves. It's like a witch's broom, magically sprouting. Ada pours a bitter-smelling tea Mitri's prepared from herbs into little coloured cups. 'Drink it quickly,' she says.

We strip. Svetlana's wonderful body glows purest white like a medieval Flemish painting.

As soon as I open the door to the steamy inner sanctum the heat blasts me full in the face. I don't know if I'll be able to bear this. The place drips humidity and I'm already breathless as I stretch out on the steamy top bench as Ada commands. She takes up the birch broom and the thrashing begins, lightly at first, up and down my body, tingling my stomach, stinging my breasts, prickling my thighs and calves and, oh unbearably, tickling my feet. I laugh hysterically.

'Please try to be serious,' says Ada, commanding me to lie on my stomach. The branches whish through the air and rustle as they hit my body. I relax, succumb to it, and the stinging sensation becomes pleasurable, not without hot pricks of pain. I suppose it's a mild version of what fetishists who like to be beaten feel.

'Do you have a bad heart?' Ada asks.

'I don't know. Why?'

'Because it is not good to take the *banya* if you have the bad heart,' she informs me, thrashing harder.

Svetlana takes over. She's ten times stronger than Ada and now the real beating begins. She really lays into me, the broom singing as it whips through the air. An albino Madame Lash. If I was gay, this would be very sexy. As I'm not, it's merely transcendental. I give myself over to the hot pain, the lacerating stings, envying masochists their ability to derive pleasure from agony. My face and body must be the colour of beetroot by now. Am I bleeding anywhere?

I grit my teeth: it's doing me good. If it goes on for much longer I'm going to have to scream.

Mercifully it stops. There's a lull and I gasp with the shock of the cold water Svetlana douses my body with. Half aware of an ecstatic tingling in my body, I sink into a stupor. I float, my consciousness in some still, removed place. I do not think I have a bad heart, I smile to myself as I lie there, oblivious.

Mitri's voice outside impinges on my bliss. He's bellowing instructions to Ada: to have the full benefit of the *banya* I must drink the herbal tea at the right time. 'Tell him to be quiet,' I mumble. 'He's spoiling my peace.'

She shrieks at him like a fishwife to shut up. I hear Vassily chortle with laughter and I drift back into the land of the long pink cloud.

'You must to get up soon,' says Ada. 'It is not good to lie there too long. If this *banya* was nearer to beach we could go out and plunge into ocean.' She throws a bucket of ice-cold water over me and I scream with shock.

'Get up now,' she commands. 'You must to have the wash and drink more tea. Take this shampoo.'

———•◦•———

Ada and I splay on benches in Mitri's garden, our backs against the wall, smiling dreamily. Every muscle in my body is relaxed. I feel elated. Idly we watch Mitri cook pork shasliks on an open fire. Ada's skin glows and I feel mine glowing too. There is no better beauty treatment than a *banya*.

I think how wonderful this aspect of Russian life is. In the west you'd pay through the nose for a health treatment like this, but there's such a deep sense of community here that those with *bani* make them available to their neighbours and they all perform the ritual for each other and it costs nothing. And the ritual itself creates even greater bonds between friends. Being naked with a person in a steamy room and having them thrash into you, and vice versa, creates an intimacy, a sense of kinship. I feel this now with Ada, this closeness.

We giggle as Felix scales the old apple tree in about two seconds and balances his way across its topmost branch, Kolbasa looking up at him, wagging his tail and yipping excitedly. Felix slips, hangs suspended from the branch by his two front paws, looks down, lets go and lands on the branch below, gripping with all his might, goggle-eyed, as it bounces beneath him, sending us into gales of laughter.

'This is such clever small cat,' giggles Ada. 'You know, Mitri found him in this place. I have not told you this story.'

'No. Tell me.'

'A man who lives near here try to drown him in the river. The mother cat had six babies and they keep for three weeks so mother doesn't get sick with the milk. Then this man put them all in a sack with the rock and ties the sack. He throw it into the middle of river and it sinks. The poor cats drown, but Felix escape. Can you believe it?'

'How?'

'We are not sure. Mitri come out here one morning when I am in Tomsk and finds Felix, so tiny, very wet and shivering. He take him inside and takes care of him. One day soon after, this man sees Mitri with Felix in the garden and he says, "Ach! This cat. I have tried to kill it twice." He try twice to drown Felix and both times he escape. I think maybe first time he goes back to his mother but he knows he must not do this again. So he find Mitri.'

'He really is a wonder cat.'

Mitri and Vassily burst out laughing.

'I am so happy for Mitri that Vassily like him so much,' says Ada.

'What do you mean? He's his father, isn't he?'

'Yes of course, but Mitri does not grow up with Vassily. He grow up here, with his grandmother in this dacha. It is very strange for a Russian to always live in the dacha; it is meant only for summer, so Mitri have strange life. Like, er … little bit wild.'

'Why didn't he live with Vassily and Novimira?'

'No, no, no,' she says frowning, lowering her voice and wagging her finger. 'Novimira does not permit Vassily to have Mitri. He is not her child. Vassily have Mitri with other woman.'

'Who? Was he married before?'

'No. He has Mitri while he is married to Novimira, so she is not so happy and does not wish Vassily to see Mitri.'

'Did she have children to Vassily?'

'No.'

'What happened to Mitri's mother?'

Ada shrugs. 'Mitri does not see her. It is Vassily's mother who loves Mitri, so she bring him up. And, you know, they never came here, Vassily and Novimira. It was so terrible for Mitri that he never saw his father. Only in last two years since his grandmother die, they start to come here and only then does Mitri begin to know his father. You know, Mitri is thirty-five and this is crazy.'

'You'd never know he's had any sadness in his life,' I say. 'Mitri never complains.' Ada gives me a look and I add, 'Well, maybe a little when he's drunk. He's never in a bad mood though. He's so sweet natured and happy. And he always wants the people around him to be happy. Why is this, do you think?'

'Maybe because he grow up in dacha surrounded by the nature and life is so simple.'

The wire door of the dacha creaks open and Novimira steps out and walks toward us, her grey curls a silver halo in the fading light. What Ada has told me cannot alter my opinion of her as dignified, kindly and gentle; but then most people mellow as they grow older.

Kolbasa runs to her, tail wagging, Felix springing after him. She bends down to pat the dog's silky head, whispering endearments to him.

'What if they wanted to take Kolbasa and put him in a rocket to the moon?' I say to her when she joins us on the bench. 'Would you let him go?'

'I am an old woman now,' she says, smiling a little sadly. 'I am finished with all of that.'

FORBIDDEN CITY

Things begin to turn full circle. Ada's ex-husband, Slava, is visiting St Petersburg. She asks if I would like to meet him. Of course. I've already had an introduction to him, of sorts. Carlotta, our mutual Australian friend, mentioned him in her first letter to me from Russia.

Each time Carlotta travelled to Russia it was at a crucial moment in its recent history: the end of the Gorbachev era, the coup, and the first year of perestroika. What Carlotta witnessed during these turbulent times made riveting reading, but that first letter, written in Tomsk in 1991, remains the most vivid of all.

It was actually a package, posted from St Petersburg (then Leningrad), containing a large book and a letter. The contrast between these two items was so startling that I still recall being captivated by the charm of the photographs in the book and the sickly feeling that crept over me as I read the letter. That moment has stayed with me — not least because the letter contains the first mention of Ada — but also because its contrast between seductive facades and veiled horrors is in so many ways a paradigm of the Russian experience.

The photographs were of the historic quarter of Tomsk, a large university city in western Siberia which dates back to 1604. Its exquisitely carved timber houses, streets of them, spoke of a storybook world of innocence and gingerbread. The letter? Here's an extract:

I'm living in the old part of Tomsk where the folk-art houses in the book are ... Natasha, the wonderful woman I've been staying with, has been so kind to me I'd be dead without her. I'm serious. I've just survived the medical terrors of a filthy, freezing, fatally under-resourced Tomsk hospital. What a place to have your appendix out. I won't bore you with the agony. Talk about Solzhenitzsyn! Forget antibiotics and anaesthetics — this place didn't have disinfectants. 'Get me on a plane to Moscow,' I screamed. 'I'm not having an operation here.' 'If you want to go to Moscow you will go in a coffin,' the surgeon told me. Apparently the system is breaking down and they're not provided with anything any more. She did her best for me, found just enough anaesthetic to give me a local, thank God, and she did a beautiful job — the wound is so neat. I've been back here at Natasha's for five days now and I can still smell the shit and piss and cabbage soup stink of that place and see the cockroaches running all over the floor. I don't know if I dreamt the rats or if they were really there. Saint Natasha spoon-fed me, washed me and slept by my bed in a stretcher every night. Now I'm as white and worn out as everyone else in this place.

There's something very mysterious going on here. Natasha's husband goes into the forest every day to get rainwater. What's this about? Until last year Tomsk was a closed city. 'Forbidden to foreigners.' When I ask them why, they point to this huge area a few kilometres out enclosed by triple electric fences with checkpoints and scary yellow signs. They also point DOWN. Spooky. When I ask what's going on, they're vague. They probably don't know. That's the way it is — they can't do anything about it. It's so IRRITATING. Everything here is 'Nichevo', but Russians are so fantastic in other ways, I keep my mouth shut. Just imagine, I arrive here alone, meet Natasha at an artists' cooperative and three weeks later she's nursing me 24 hours a day as if I'm her dearest child.

I'll try to calm down and tell you everything in order. I'm still weak and bedridden but as soon as I can stand up I'm out of here in one of their antique planes.

Ten days later

I can walk. All is explained. Some of it anyway. I've made a new friend called Ada who works in the art museum here. She's the wife of Slava, the handsome man *who organised my exhibition in Omsk and helped me repair my paintings. The KGB slashed them all when I arrived at Moscow airport, looking for 'concealed goods'. They interrogated me for hours. They said anyone who would come all the way from Australia to exhibit their paintings in Russia where nobody has any money to buy them would have to be mad. In the end I think they finally let me go because they decided I <u>was</u> mad. Ada has contacts for me to exhibit in Leningrad. I'm leaving here as soon as she can get me a ticket.*

She told me the reason so many people get sick here is that the water is badly contaminated. Her mother is a doctor and, as she said, the only people in Tomsk who know anything are the doctors, the scientists and the workers at Tomsk-7 — the forbidden city behind the barbed wire. It's huge apparently, partly underground. It's all so dark and creepy.

Yesterday I had such an eerie experience with Ada. She took me to the Tomsk cemetery and showed me all these graves of women and babies. She explained that from the dates on the headstones you could work out that the women had died in childbirth or soon after, and that the babies were newborn or up to a week old. I asked what was going on but she shrugged off my questions. Either she's very close or scared or she doesn't know. We walked among the graves, some of them so tiny, and there were so many of them. Eventually we just stood there,

speechless. It was overwhelmingly sad. Maybe there was
something personal in all this for Ada but my strongest
feeling was that she'd taken me there because she thought
of me somehow as a witness.

Tomsk-7 remains a closed city. Its activities, however, are no longer a secret. Behind its triple electric wire fences, now falling into disrepair, the cooling towers of military-grade plutonium-producing reactors loom against the sky like giant metal beehives. Liquid radioactive waste from its inadequate storage facilities has for decades been pumped down into the depths of the earth or dumped into the Tom River, resulting in a litany of ecological disasters ranging from radioactive moose and hares to contamination of waters as distant as the Arctic Ocean. Several alarming accidents and explosions have occurred there, leading to recent court actions.

Tomsk-7 was the chief producer of the Societ Union's nuclear weapons, a legacy of the Cold War and the nuclear arms race, so it seems ironic that America and Russia have come together to decide its fate — which they have been deliberating for more than five years. Although the city of Tomsk and the Siberian Chemical Combine that operates the facility fatuously insist that 'negative information about the plant is plotted by foreign commercial competitors', US and Russian scientists agree that the degree of radioactive contamination in the River Tom is the highest in the world and that Tomsk-7 is 'an environmental time bomb'.

Ada rarely speaks of her past and never of Tomsk. It's been seven years since she escaped there, when, with Tamara's support, she was appointed to the staff of the Russian Museum. I've never mentioned her journey to the graveyard with Carlotta, over ten years ago now. Her reasons for taking an outsider there as a witness have become perfectly clear. For the past six years information about Tomsk-7 — now referred to by its pre-war name of Seversk — has become readily available: reports, articles and news items detail horrifying facts and figures about 'the most radioactive waste dump in Russia'.

Curiously absent from all this is any mention of the welfare of the half a million human inhabitants of Tomsk.

High mortality rates, the death of women from childbirth, infertility, and the ongoing gynaecological problems which have blighted Ada's life, evidently do not carry sufficient weight to bring human considerations into the picture, much less the constant headaches, nausea, faintness, tiredness and paleness suffered by the people of Tomsk, or the fact that fish purchased in a Tomsk market have radiation levels twenty times higher than normal.

What about an accident? Would that do it?

On 6 April 1993 a violent explosion ripped through a uranium tank, destroying two floors of the Combine's chemical separation plant, resulting in radioactive contamination of the village of Georgievka on the outskirts of Tomsk-7. The explosion was caused by the storage of French waste fuel in a plant with technical capabilities designed only for Russian fuel. Numerous accidents had occurred previously — there have been twenty-three in all. They resulted in several lawsuits initiated by Tomsk environmentalist groups. Some of these have gone as far as the Supreme Court. All have been unsuccessful. The 1993 explosion of Tomsk-7 is having an unprecedented outcome: twenty-six Georgievka villagers have filed a lawsuit against the Siberian Chemical Combine. This is the first time individuals have brought a class action. Naturally it has taken years to be processed.

The twenty-six Georgievkian claimants demand two things: compensation for what is euphemistically described as 'moral damage' caused by radioactive contamination of their village, and that the Combine cease dumping liquid radio-active waste underground.

Since filing the suit fourteen of the claimants have died.

The court is scheduled to hear the case in a few weeks.

———•◦•———

Ada's past and her life in Tomsk have come to visit her, in the shape of her ex-husband. We arrange to meet in the Summer Garden at 12.30.

The day can't make up its mind, the sun beaming one minute, moody clouds amassing the next. By the time I round the granite curve of the Winter Canal and turn into Nevsky — to be greeted by the astonishing sight of a procession solemnly wending its way the prospekt's entire length — tufts of cloud drift like smoke signals above. Bearing street-wide banners and gowned head to foot in purest white with pointed caps, from this distance the processional figures look ominously Inquisitional. I assume their tidings are religious. The Russian Orthodox Church is back in a big way.

As I draw closer to the marchers, I see that their gowns are in fact zippered overalls and that the majority of them are bright, youngish and worried looking, not fusty old church types. With a white-gloved hand, one of them offers me a loaf of bread and a parcel wrapped in paper marked with nuclear hazard stickers. Accepting the parcel and feeling that it's a brick, I smilingly return it.

I arrive in the Summer Garden a few minutes late. As I walk along sun-dappled paths under arching branches I catch sight of Ada and presumably Slava together on a park bench and immediately hide, my back to a large tree so that they can't see me nor I them. It's not just the privacy of the moment, the way they lean toward each other wrapped in intimacy, it's my astonishment at suddenly seeing Ada, without any forewarning that this would be the case, with her perfect male complement.

Five minutes later I sit talking and laughing with them. My first impression proves correct. Slava's very blue eyes are quick and kind, his longish brown hair poetic. Like Ada his bone structure is delicate, his air vulnerable but alert. He's handsome, clever, educated, interested in everything in the world: Ada's intellectual equal.

This morning I've been to the little art nouveau bookshop near the Moika Canal. Ada insists on looking at the books I've bought. 'Ooh,' she says, turning over an erotic French novel. She flicks through its pages and smilingly shows it to Slava, and I can see that, in her demure way, she welcomes the opportunity to share an erotic moment with him once again.

I recall Carlotta telling me of Slava's drunken histrionics when he followed Ada to St Petersburg after she'd left Tomsk, how he'd thrown himself in the snow, wailing in despair, and how Ada had stood looking down at him, her face like stone and her heart like ice, as Carlotta with her tendency to melodrama described it.

I wonder about the contradiction between this and what I've just witnessed in the Summer Garden. I wonder why they divorced.

I ask Slava, who speaks a little English, whether he saw the protest on Nevsky Prospekt and knows what's going on.

Between them he and Ada tell me that it's an antinuclear protest. The protesters' offerings are symbolic, the bricks ironically representing the nuclear waste Russia accepts as a 'gift' from other countries, and the loaves of bread 'compensation' for taking the waste. For decades now, Russia has been storing the nuclear waste of other countries (France isn't the only opportunist). The government is reaping considerable income from the storage fees and now wishes to significantly expand the enterprise by building several new storage facilities at Tomsk, the Kuril Islands and three other sites.

'And when I tell you where is one of these new sites, you won't believe me,' says Ada.

'Novgorod,' I guess, thinking the worst would be the desecration of Russia's oldest and holiest city.

'No. Here. Just outside of St Petersburg.'

What can I say? Is this the latest chapter in Moscow's age-old will to destroy upstart, European St Petersburg?

The government also proposes to lease Russian land to countries for their nuclear waste storage, until the half-life of the element has expired. 'This make for a very long lease,' says Ada, 'because Slava want me particularly to tell you that half-life of uranium is one hundred and fifty thousand years.'

In a few weeks the Russian duma will reconvene to decide the issue. Russians want it put to a referendum, but before the government will agree to do this, it requires a petition with a minimum of two million signatures.

I want to get back to the protest to see what's going on. My departure will also allow Ada and Slava a little more time alone together. I say my farewells.

'Don't forget you must allow the time to dress for Mariinsky Theatre tonight,' Ada yells after me.

⋆

Nevsky Prospekt is choked with protesters and banners, Greenpeace's the only one I recognise among the environmental and human rights groups. I push through the crowd, ears alert for the sound of English being spoken. Ten minutes of shoving and being shoved and I find an oracle of sorts: a British film crew interviewing an English-speaking Russian.

'I'm against building new storage facilities near St Petersburg, where I and my children will live,' the man says into the mike. 'Turning a great historical centre into a nuclear cemetery isn't smart. It was bad enough when trains from Finland loaded with nuclear waste used to travel through here on their way to Mayak. Those trains are still backed up twenty kilometres. Duma member Klimov says the money from storage can solve Russia's financial problems, but our lives are worth more than money. Not one person working at a nuclear power station agrees with Klimov because they know how many accidents there have been.'

'More storage facilities mean more accidents,' a woman yells.

The man continues: 'If the import of more nuclear waste becomes legal, life in Russia will become very dangerous. Companies will try to save money on safety and will do illegal deals. It's inevitable.'

Later, this man, whose name is Marek, tells me that at present Russia has a nuclear waste load equivalent to 120 Chernobyls.

'Most governments have only contempt for the people they govern,' is his parting comment. 'But nowhere more so than in Russia.'

Ada and I are currently being subjected to some Russian contempt of a more personal kind. We're sitting alone in the vast nineteenth century main dining room of the Metropole restaurant, its palms, parquetry and Corinthian columns a reminder of just how grand and cosmopolitan St Petersburg was in pre-Soviet times. There's even an orchestra platform at one end, but the Cole Porter playing now is coming from speakers. I'm treating Ada to dinner here before we go to the Mariinsky Ballet tonight.

Ada often strikes me as a provincial in St Petersburg. Outside her home and place of work, she has no favourite haunts, no special place to go for a quiet drink or meeting with a friend. Yet this is nothing to do with her being a provincial; Tamara's the same. On their low income the price of a cup of coffee's prohibitive, and, besides, cafe society has not yet been embraced into the Russian lifestyle. Whenever we eat in a restaurant, Ada is uncomfortable.

At the Metropole's marble entrance she was distinctly reluctant: 'No. It will be too expensive. Let's go to ...' but I persuaded her. The maitre d' when we entered was surly, so was the attendant in the cloakroom at the top of the sweeping marble stairs; and the present manner of the rigid-backed waiter as he deposits our chicken Kiev and Russian salad with boiled eggs in front of us is so haughty I could give him a good slap.

'In Soviet times women could not go to the restaurant

without the man,' says Ada when the waiter goes off to get a bottle of Moldavian wine. 'It's changing a little bit now. When first I come here it was with Carlotta, when she come to Russia second time. As we go up steps, man at front door step outside and say we cannot go in. Carlotta say to me, "Why?" and when this man hear that Carlotta speak the English he change his mind and say, "Ooh, please come in," and open the door.'

'Why wouldn't he have let you in if you'd both been Russian?' I ask.

'They think the Russian women alone are the prostitutes. Many men dine here and they think the women come to find the man.'

I look around at the grand room, deserted but for the two of us. Yet another shell of an extinguished way of life, another St Petersburg time warp. The Nabokov family might have eaten here; certainly it would have been a favourite with artists and the intelligentsia. The Metropole would then have looked as it does now, except for its present aura of being long dead, its palpable sense of absence.

'What do you think about?' asks Ada.

'About what a strange day it's been,' I answer.

It has indeed: an emotional one for Ada and an eye-opening one for me.

'Slava is so sensitive and handsome,' I say. 'Why did you divorce him?'

'Because he tell me he will come to St Petersburg, but he does not. For two years I wait for him, and he never comes.'

'It would have been difficult for him to get a job here, wouldn't it? One as good as being the director of the art museum in Omsk?'

'No, it is not for this reason he does not come,' she sniffs.

'Why then?' I ask as I refill our glasses with the ruby wine.

'You know, I marry Slava in Tomsk. I grow up in that place but many things that happen there are bad luck for me. Allow me to give you the example. Tomsk has many beautiful things, the library has jewelled books and the university is oldest in Siberia and very good. They say the education there is more liberal than in other parts of Russia, but when I am a student there we are made to go out in fields and dig potatoes in freezing ground, for weeks, and we are not paid — very hard work and why must students be made to do this? At art museum in Tomsk, after I put up the exhibitions, every time I must to telephone Soviet authority and he come and look before launch and say if exhibition can stay on the walls or not. Sometimes I must to take it down.' She frowns deeply. 'Tomsk is ... big black cloud in my life. Bad things happen always there. My mother is doctor but must work in bad Soviet job and is not old but now she is sick for such a long time. I think maybe she ...' she looks away and shakes her head sorrowfully, 'does not recover. My brother? Pfff! My first husband Yuri ...' She shrugs and breaks off.

'Tell me about Yuri,' I say, remembering she'd once referred to him. 'What happened with him?'

She shrugs again. 'Yuri was a poet, very good and good musician too. We were very young and at first we are like happy children. He came from very good family — his father was Professor of Philology at Tomsk University — but he liked vodka, really too much. I try to save the money for the small apartment but always Yuri wants to go out and have the party and drink the vodka. I feel big passion for Yuri but I cannot stay with him. So I divorce him and save for apartment myself and he is free to drink the vodka. But always I am sad for him, even after I marry Slava. Yuri was … It was so terrible waste. He breaks his parents' heart.

'One morning, after I come to St Petersburg, I receive desperate telephone call from his father. Yuri has been found in small dark alley stabbed many times. Murdered. Nobody knows why this happen. They can never find out who did this. It was terrible. Afterwards his parents are very kind to me and, when I divorce from Slava also, they help me.'

'My god, Ada, what sad things you've survived.' We sit silently. I pour the remainder of the wine into our glasses. 'Here's to you for escaping Tomsk,' I say, raising my glass. She smiles as we click glasses, her eyes glittering and her pale cheeks a little flushed from the wine, and briefly she looks much younger and I can see how trusting she must once have been.

'And here's to Yuri,' I add. Poor Yuri. I can picture Ada's resolve when she decided to leave him, her determination to build a secure world for herself and have an apartment of her own. She can't have been more than twenty-two. Do I know a woman stronger than Ada? Do I know a *man* stronger than Ada?

'Will you ever tell me why you divorced Slava?' I ask.

'Yes, of course, my darling, if you must know,' she smiles, and tells me how every weekend after they were married Slava would rush back to her in Tomsk and how happy they were. They didn't live together during the week because he worked in Omsk, a two-hour train ride away. Ada was pleased with this arrangement because by this time she was working in the Tomsk museum and had saved very hard and bought a tiny one-room apartment.

It would have been around this time that Carlotta met Ada, on her memorable first trip to Russia.

'Was Slava happy to see you only on weekends?' I ask.

She hesitates. 'Not so much. Maybe yes and no. Slava is not so happy with everything because he would love to live with all of his family all the time and he can't do this. He love me very much but can only see me two, maybe one day a week. He love his children very much and can see them only,' she shrugs, 'once a week maybe. I don't know. Most of the time he lives alone.'

'Slava has children?' He'd seemed too poetic for fatherhood.

'Yes, He married Tartar woman at first. When they divorce he is very upset he won't live with his children. As time goes on he worries more about this. And you know, Slava is so unhappy because he doesn't live with me and so unhappy he doesn't live with his children that, you know, he can't make up his mind what to do. He is not so strong.'

'Is this why he didn't follow you to St Petersburg? Because he would never have seen his children?'

'Maybe,' she says quietly.

'Oh, that's so terrible,' I say. 'It's because Russia is so huge. Siberia and St Petersburg — it's another world. And you told me yourself that plane fares to Tomsk are so expensive. What a decision to make. You can't blame him, Ada.'

'After waiting such long time I understood that someone must to make this decision,' she says coldly.

Ah, she does blame him. She's never forgiven him.

I think of what Carlotta said — a face of stone and a heart of ice. The expression on Ada's face as she looked down at Slava that day must have been like the one she's wearing now.

'We must leave straightaway for the Mariinsky or we will be late,' she says, looking at her watch.

We catch a trolleybus along quiet old canal streets to Teatralnaya Ploshchad and there in all its peppermint-green and white baroque splendour is the home of the Kirov Ballet.

The crowded foyer's abuzz, the mood effervescent. Ada's so excited that she managed to get tickets for *Les Sylphides*. She's paid the Russian price of 1000 rubles for each of them, so now I must pretend I'm Russian, other wise I'll have to fork out god knows how much for the 'tourist price'.

'Just say *pazhalsta*. Nothing else,' warns Ada.

'Yes, I know,' I say. Even from this far back in the queue I can hear that's what the natives are saying as they go through the Russian checkpoint up ahead presided over by Stalin's female double.

'God, you can't even go to the ballet here without having a KGB experience,' I whinge to Ada.

'Sh,' she whispers, annoyed. 'You must not speak the English.'

I relax. The way to bring this off is to do it casually. It's so important to Ada. She wants this trip to the ballet to be her treat; I can tell she's carefully put the money aside. The tourist price would be way beyond her means, so if I don't pass the upcoming little test it means disappointing her.

We reach the top of the queue.

'*Pazhalsta*,' I say nonchalantly and professionally and Stalinovna clicks the ticket and scans my face as she hands it back and I know I've made it. I'm on my way through. She thinks I'm a Russian. Yippee. I smile at her and as soon as I do this I know it's a fatal mistake. I keep going anyway and behind me all hell breaks loose. Stalinovna sounds like she looks.

I turn back. It's a lost cause.

I go back downstairs to the tourist ticket box, pay the staggering price of 225,000 rubles (about $100) for my ticket, join a different queue to enter the theatre and somehow, after Ada negotiates with two or three people, end up sitting next to her.

She's mortified by the price of my ticket. I try to hide it from her but she grabs it, saying, 'Russian government think all people who come here are Americans.' I start oohing and aahing about the decor to get her mind off it. She loves me to praise St Petersburg. The theatre with its dizzying tiers of gilded balconies is wonderful. So is the antique hand-painted theatre curtain, a *trompe l'oeil* extravaganza of loops, garlands and twirls in blues and greens. As I babble on a smile takes over her face.

'What?' I ask.

'In Metropole they let us in because you speak the English. In Mariinsky they don't let you in because you speak the English. I worry you must think Russia is very crazy place.'

'But this is why we love it,' I say.

I'm no fan of ballet, but even I can appreciate the intricate skill of the prima ballerina, her soufflé lightness. It's breathtaking. She never comes off her toes; the footwork's so fast her feet blur. At one point she toe dances on air. I glance at Ada. She's enraptured.

———◆·◆·◆———

Outside, the day's restless clouds have finally amassed to produce a downpour. Giggling, we run across the road to the Irish pub, where I introduce Ada to Guinness. She can't get over how black it is but seems to enjoy it.

We emerge into dark silent streets slicked with rain, street lamps making eerie pools of light. Passing palaces and elegant period houses, we follow the Moika River to Nevsky Prospekt and catch the trolleybus home.

Ada sits next to a window and looks out into the blackness. In the glass I see the ghost of her reflection, fine blonde hair a halo above strong bones and set mouth, her green eyes faintly smudged with tiredness.

If she'd been able to have a child with Slava, perhaps he would have followed her to St Petersburg.

As if reading my thoughts, she turns to me. 'I am thinking about Slava and Yuri. These are interesting men for me when I am young. Mitri is more special man now that I am older.'

'You're starting to love Mitri, aren't you?'

She turns to look outside and doesn't reply. I see her reflection smiling in the window.

———•◦•———

The lawsuit of the twenty-six Georgievka claimants, only twelve of whom remain alive, finally comes before the courts.

The court admits that the explosion at Tomsk-7 caused serious 'moral injury' by its radioactive contamination of Georgievka. It orders the Siberian Chemical Combine to pay each claimant compensation of US$860.

With regard to the pumping of radioactive waste down to 500 metres under the earth, the court finds the Tomsk administration not responsible. The claimants point out that such large-scale underground dumping contradicts Russian legislation, but even so, the court's decision is ratified by Russia's Nuclear State Regulatory. The ruling is further endorsed when the Russian Prime Minister, Mikhail Kasyanov, signs a decree granting the Siberian Chemical Combine the right to dump liquid radio-active waste into underground water-bearing horizons.

At last I comprehend Tamara's insistence that there is no law in Russia. The machinery of the law exists — lawyers, courts, county courts, the Supreme Court, due legal process — but it's so eroded by corruption and long habits of contempt for individual human rights that it's barely functional.

PETROZAVODSK POST

The night train speeds northeast toward Murmansk, into the heartland of Old Russia. Tomorrow we sail to the island of Kizhi where this way of life is preserved, but first we must stop at Petrozavodsk; Tamara has some business at the art museum.

Tamara and I have a sleeping compartment to ourselves. We make up our beds with their coarse grey blankets and curious sheets like thick tissue paper. I've spent the day traipsing Nevsky Prospekt photographing my favourite buildings — I leave in ten days — and I'm tired. Nevertheless, I agree with Tamara that it's impossible to sleep on trains and we curl up opposite each other, talking. She leans across and turns on the night-light. There's the fizzling sound of a faulty connection as the amber light slowly glows into being, then fades, again brightens, slowly peters out and rekindles. On and off it goes, like a drunken neon sign.

'Ada tells me you've settled into your new apartment,' I

say. 'You must be relieved to have that terrible worry out of your life.'

She pulls a distasteful face. 'I tell you Russian saying: "We make fairytales a reality. We make Kafka a reality." This is clever pun because Russian word for reality is *shaska*, but you understand meaning anyway. And moving to new apartment for me is like punishment for committing crime I did not know I have committed.'

'Is the apartment so terrible?'

'You will see,' she says with a curious mix of anger and resignation.

As if deflecting her personal anger, she launches into a monologue about the Soviet suppression of artists, bitterly relating the fate of the great modernist painter, Pavel Filanov, who died of starvation in the freezing St Petersburg winter of 1941. Tamara is well versed on Filanov's life: she wrote the thick Filanov monograph and curated the exhibition of his works that toured Europe and Britain in the early nineties. Filanov's paintings are like enormous shattered jewels — full of explosive vitality, insistently spiritual, increasingly neurotic.

'Soviet authorities did not always persecute directly,' she says. 'Sometimes they got at those they marked out by terrorising their families or people around them. For example, Stalin try to destroy Akhmatova by executing her husband and sending her son to labour camp.'

The night-light waxes and wanes erratically. As Tamara speaks, I'm constantly aware of it on my right.

'In Filanov's case they do both. They persecute him and watch him starve but they also get at him by tormenting his students. One young man they keep interrogating about Filanov's formalism. Such stupid interrogations. Mindless. They make you crazy. One day authorities interrogate this student again, and when they leave he commit suicide.'

Her eyes are brimming with tears. She must have told this story countless times. Does she become so furious and upset every time she tells it? I don't think so. Yes, twentieth century painting is her specialty and it's only natural that she takes the fates of her artists so personally. And I know she's telling me this terrible story so that people outside Russia will know of the horrors of life under Stalin. Nonetheless, in the controlled rage in her voice I sense a subtext, a personal one — long-suppressed emotions, associated with the Soviet bullying of her dead husband perhaps — and current rage, despair, at the injustice of being forced to leave her beloved apartment. She belonged in that apartment. Such a majestic, cultivated woman whose life is devoted to the cultural history of St Petersburg deserves to live in a piece of that history. She knows I believe this; I've said as much to her. So I am a sympathetic ear for this sudden release of emotion which, disguised as it may be, is out of character for Tamara. I'm the perfect ear in fact; I'm a visitor and I'm leaving soon.

I wish I could comfort her in some way. I search my mind for something to say but all I can come up with is the 'look on the bright side, you have such a wonderful job' kind of patter that will be no comfort at all.

The irritating night-light is giving me a headache. I turn it off and we're plunged into darkness. The train has increased its speed and we're flying along. I'm becoming sleepy but Tamara now embarks on a story about Kasimir Malevich and I listen with horrified fascination to how Russia's Ministry of Culture seized ownership of nearly all of Malevich's artworks in Russia, defrauding his poverty-stricken grand-daughter of her inheritance, now worth billions. It is indeed a Kafka-esque tale of the machinations of a faceless bureaucracy, chilling in its utter contempt for artists and their families; yet it has at the same time a plot so absurd that it might have been co-authored by Gogol.

I'm falling asleep, wondering whether Tamara has really told me all this or I'm dreaming it, when Tamara says, 'Imagine Notary's Office in 1935 categorising Malevich's paintings as worthless when already he is famous in Europe. This is example for you of how Soviet criminals have their origins as imbeciles.' She's turned that annoying light on again to fossick for something in her bag, so I know I'm still awake.

Petrozavodsk is the capital of the Karelian Republic and is flat swampland like St Petersburg but has none of its architectural magic. Its largely 1940s buildings are grey, grim, shabby examples of the Stalinist style. It is cold, bleak and largely featureless except for a giant statue of Lenin gesticulating angrily. It is one of the most depressing cities I've ever been in. It embodies all the drabness of Stalinism; indeed it is still a conservative Soviet stronghold.

Its art museum with its peeling white paint is the world's ugliest, although it has a fine collection of icons. The interior is chilly, more like a town hall than an art gallery. The museum's new director, Tamara tells me sniffily, is an ex-Soviet Party official. I gather she's not exactly an art scholar. Today is her first day on the job.

Here she comes down the stairs to greet us, a shortish, dark curly-haired, curvaceous woman in a figure-hugging navy suit. She's utterly charismatic — three or four members of staff buzz around her like drones at a queen bee — and more than delighted to see Tamara and welcome a visitor from Australia. She has the kind of smile — and she beams at everyone and everything nonstop — that you know will remain fixed as she cheerfully eliminates any obstacle to her objectives.

Tamara disappears into the rabbit warren of downstairs rooms to attend to her curatorial affairs. The new director and her attendants, exclaiming how exciting it is that the Hermitage is to stage an exhibition of Australian Aboriginal art, sweep me up and along corridors to a large, dark space at the back of the museum. In her excellent English the new director introduces me to 'one of our conceptual artists — very modern with an interest in international movements' and then sweeps off with her entourage.

'My name is Pavel,' says the handsome young artist with a knowing smile. He then treats me to flourishes of tattered paint-splashed canvases, drawn from a stack on the floor, which he has physically attacked in various ways. He holds each one up for me to admire, then chucks it back on the floor. The canvasses are expressively painted and some of them are very large — and very mauled, slashed, rubbish-flicked and, it appears, driven over at high speed. This must be his private war with art, I think.

'You're a good painter,' I say. 'I understand you want to go beyond that but it's kind of a waste.'

'Waste? All art is waste in Russia,' he responds. 'Maybe it's not so bad if you work in Moscow or St Petersburg, but for artists like us who live in the provinces, it is impossible.' Pavel explains to me that his despoiled canvases are a statement against the Russian government for forbidding works of art to leave the country. He wraps up these blatantly nonprecious works and posts them to various countries in defiance of this law.

I wonder what the new director would think of this; she's gone off to give a press conference.

Pavel insists I meet his friend, Arcady, whom he keeps referring to as 'Russia's best artist'. 'There's an opening at the museum tonight and my friend will be here. Why don't you come?'

I tell him the exhibiting artist's a friend of Tamara's and we were coming in any case.

Having met a few painters in St Petersburg, I've seen that since perestroika things haven't improved for Russian artists. The torment has merely become more generalised and less personal than under Stalin, taking the form of criminal neglect and the formulation of ever more inane government policies regarding the sale of art. In one way the situation is much worse. In Soviet times, if an artist toed the line, he could become well off, respected, a darling of Party figures. Not so now, as there is no longer any line to toe. Sure, it's good that they can now paint, sculpt, conceive what and how they like, but, deprived by Stalin of the bridging stages of late modernism, Russian artists are all at sea, grappling with, bewildered by, the complexities of postmodernism. Installations are in vogue, as they are everywhere. I wonder what kind of work Arcady does.

———◦◦◦———

Shortly after lunch Tamara and I escape the art museum and Petrozavodsk. As soon as we sail across Lake Onega to Kizhi Island, the sun comes out.

I lie on my back in emerald-green grass in an ecstasy of silent, sweet-smelling solitude, looking up at the twenty-two silver minarets of the ancient Cathedral of the Transfiguration glimmering against the bright blue heavens. This is Holy Russia.

The breathtaking cathedral with its clusters of fairytale minarets, their carved timbers silvered by time, overlooks two small villages at either end of the island. They cluster in a landscape of rustically fenced farm animals and windmills with the blue lake beyond.

The cathedral's doors are closed; it was built in 1714 and is delicate. Constructed without using a single nail, in an ingenious way that keeps rain off the walls, opinions on how to restore it differ and work has been deferred. But look at the cathedral and these facts evaporate. It's sublime, the Chartres of the Russian vernacular.

Like the proverbial Russian soul and peasant culture that Tolstoy so idealised, Kizhi is partly — only partly — an invention. In order to conserve the exquisite timber peasants' houses with their elaborate carving, some have been transported here from other regions around Lake Onega. At Kizhi the peasant culture of Old Russia which was all but obliterated by the Soviets is preserved — its rustic architecture, Byzantine-style icons, folk embroidery and masterpieces of woodcarving. A fourteenth century church, the oldest remaining wooden building in Russia, houses icons dark with age and shimmering with gold. Traditional village life is also preserved; the houses in one of the hamlets are occupied year-round by the island's inhabitants.

In the sun and silence the island seems deserted. Apart from the inhabitants and Tamara and me, it is. So far in the north, so far east of St Petersburg, it is as remote from contemporary Russia as the way of life it preserves, and people rarely visit here.

I walk down the hill along the winding path toward an imposing two-storey house built of dark logs, the external staircase, balconies and windows with their shutters all elaborately carved in paler wood. No nails have been used in these buildings either, nor in the unusual fences of diagonal timbers. A rich peasant would have owned this house. It's beautiful, of course, but stern and stolid compared with the ethereal lightness of the cathedral.

Tamara's inside the house talking with its elderly occupant. The downstairs windows are small, probably to keep out cold during the freezing winters; from the great

arched entrance I walk into gloom. The smiling old woman with her bright headscarf and hand-knitted green cardigan rises and hands me a bunch of yellow wildflowers. She threads my arm through hers and leads me upstairs, through a heavy panelled door stained rich indigo, and proudly shows me the large kitchen at the back.

What a joy it must be to cook here. Light streams in from the many windows recessed into the thick walls. No matter where I stand there is a vista of the lake below, of soft carpets of grass with linden trees and munching horses and cattle. In a corner of the kitchen is an enormous white brick stove with ornamental arches; it nearly reaches the high ceiling. Around the walls run rough shelves containing traditional blue and white china, iron pans, hand-carved ladles and cooking utensils, and gleaming silver and brass samovars, the first I've seen outside an antique shop.

'Would she make us some tea in a samovar?' I ask Tamara.

Delighted, the old woman, Anna, obliges.

We sit at an adzed table under one of the windows, sipping the stewed, sugary tea and admiring the ancient carved toys Anna brings over to show us: a miniature sleigh, a bell tower, a windmill and a rocking horse. Her grandfather made these, she tells us proudly, so, so long ago.

I ask Anna how she spends her days. My question sparks a sustained outburst in Russian, a rhythmical wailing, musical as a dirge. Tamara allows her to finish, which takes some considerable time, before presenting me with a summary in

English. There are the animals to feed and attend to, the cows to milk, the cheese and yogurt to make, the wood to chop, the house to keep clean, so much to do and she's getting too old for it. Her eyes are bad but she still manages some embroidery, outside, by the light of the afternoon sun. She's here alone but she keeps it all going nevertheless. What else would she do with her life? Her children left long ago, gone to live in the cities, but not her. Never. She grew up here. The village was crowded with people then and sometimes its deserted air makes her feel sad now. These days she's not so much the mother of the house, more like the keeper of a museum. And that's what Kizhi Island has become, a museum. Yes, the

cathedral is beautiful, but it's just a building. What is a cathedral without its Russian Orthodox priest with his black robes and long beard? What is a cathedral without its singing and liturgies and holy icons? The cathedral's icons are now in the Petrozavodsk art museum. What good do they do there? An icon is a gateway. Meditate on its image when you pray and you will be lifted up into a holy sphere. How can this happen in an art museum?

We commiserate, but then she smiles and tells us she knows how lucky she is to live in such a peaceful world.

As we walk to the boat landing Anna stands outside the house and waves us goodbye, a wizened, diminutive figure growing ever more distant in her verdant village landscape.

Tamara and I stand at the stern of the departing ship looking back at the island, the Cathedral of the Transfiguration and its fantastical minarets rising like a vision in a dream.

———•◦•———

Back to Petrozavodsk and contemporary Russian life. Tonight, the art museum is welcoming; it's packed with people attending the exhibition opening. For all their woes, the Russians are masters of conviviality and this opening is awash with enthusiastic congratulations and good wishes. Valudi, the exhibiting artist, is a colourist and the downstairs galleries are vibrant with his sensuous landscape paintings. He is surrounded by a crush of admirers and well-wishers. Everyone has brought him a flower.

Thinking of what Anna said this afternoon, I go upstairs to look at the icons from Kizhi. It's deserted up here, a rich and silent Byzantine world of staring faces and gesturing figures, intimate individual icons and entire narrative cycles, panel after large panel. I stare long at an ancient and strangely beautiful one, the Christ child in the Virgin's lap as if he's still in the womb. Its other unusual feature is the miniature pink angels that hover on either side of the Virgin's face. I wonder if it's a version of the Annunciation; I've no idea of its true meaning. I am struck above all by its abstract qualities as a painting, its warm, muted colours and glimmering gold. Staring into it, I can see how its very serenity could have the power to draw the beholder into its world, but I can't gain access to that world, whether because of my unfamiliarity with Orthodox traditions or my absence of belief, I don't know.

I go back downstairs just as the new director, sparkling in ice-blue polyester with crossover bodice and power shoulders, indicates it's time for official proceedings to begin. Pavel, still wearing his worn plaid flannel shirt, waves to me across the room and catches up as we mount the red-carpeted stairs in the large cream-painted foyer, a tacky chandelier overhead. Pavel tells me Arcady will arrive soon.

Two staircases, a left and a right, branch off the broad landing. Both are packed and we come to a standstill. I look up. A television crew is positioned at the railing of the floor above, camera trained on the landing. The launch is to take place on the stairs to enable all of us to see the proceedings. We make room, allowing the official party to arrange themselves on the landing, Valudi, with his leonine head and mane of grey-streaked hair, formally dressed in a pale grey suit, in the centre.

The speeches are mercifully short, each punctuated by a floral presentation and an anecdote, a song or a poem. Anyone who feels like performing in praise of the artist simply does so, spontaneously. A beaming Valudi, balancing several large bouquets, is showered with more flowers, more tributes; it's utterly chaotic and joyous, everyone laughing, shouting, clapping, stamping, singing along. An opera singer's sublime performance of one of those heartbreaking Russian dirges brings the official launch to a close.

Now for the real party. Tamara, majestic tonight in scooped-neck plum wool, leads me through the crowd to an intimate room at the back of the museum. A large table laden with food and drink dominates the room. An endless round of vodka toasts begins, to the artist's life, to his work, to the individual members of his family and, one by one, to his friends. As we leave with Pavel and Arcady an hour or so later, the company is solemnly, if a little drunkenly, drinking a toast to the artist's cat.

I was shocked on first meeting Arcady, but managed to conceal it I think. When he was seven years old he stood on a land mine. The right side of his body is smashed — his arm blown out of its socket, his eye gone, his leg badly crippled. His manner is quiet, withdrawn, but his gaze arresting, perhaps because his one eye is so very blue, so very sharp. Arcady is, of all things, a master etcher, one of the most difficult and physically demanding of all artistic processes. Or, rather, he was a master etcher. He now paints. He has relinquished etching not because of his physical disabilities (I don't think it would occur to him to allow himself to be impeded by those), but by the gradual process of erosion of spirit that Russia inflicts on its gifted artists.

In the car on the way to his studio he says to me, 'Now you will see how a Russian artist lives.'

After two months I've grown used to the putrid squalor of Russian tenement buildings. The knack is to simply shut down all your senses — particularly sight, smell and touch — until you are right inside the apartment. There you can function normally again in a clean, safe, occasionally charming environment — albeit a cluttered one.

Arcady's interior offers no such deliverance. Not that he's dirty or messy. On the contrary, he strives to maintain what order he can. But it takes a certain basic level of income to keep squalor at bay. Besides, in a room two-thirds the size of the average Australian bedroom, it's impossible to have designated spaces for eating, sleeping, sitting, working and storage of a life's work. Half the room, floor to ceiling, is given over to the latter. A narrow bed, where Tamara and I sit, and a small table occupy the rest. There's just enough space for Arcady to select works from stacks and boxes and place them on his easel to show me.

I don't know if Arcady is Russia's best artist, as Pavel claims. His concerns are so different from those of artists in the west that I'm riveted by his work's exotic nature. What I do know is that his dark, strange images are masterworks of technical virtuosity. Russians still place a heavy emphasis on mastering the craft of one's art, something that has, regrettably, been lost in the west. Skill in drawing is paramount. Arcady devoted twelve years to studying the rigorous disciplines in Russian art schools, and it shows.

Instinctively, I respond to the poetry and symbolism of Arcady's etchings, which appear to be steeped in Jungian philosophy. Yes, he has read Jung extensively, adding dismissively that you don't have to read about these things to know them. The soul, the creative intelligence, knows them anyway. Very Russian. (So much for Stalin banning Jung and practically every other western intellectual from the libraries.) Arcady's archetypes are those of fertility, birth and nurturing. (The Mother, Matrushka, will never go away in Russian culture, as it has in ours. Woman is still revered, not socially, but at a primal level.) But some unseen, unknowable evil is omnipresent in these vital images, invisibly sapping their very marrow. It doesn't lurk or swoop; it has infiltrated. It isn't the cycle of birth, decay and death that occurs in natural life processes, which inevitably arcs on to fertilisation and rebirth. This insidious evil is some horror, something alien to life, waging a silent, inevitably triumphant war upon it. An interpretive critic could have a field day with Arcady's etchings. Obviously they are at the same time historical — about Russia — and universal — about the fate of the earth. And they are also, without doubt, autobiographical. Arcady's art is a metaphor for his fate as an artist.

He shows me his paintings, beginning with the earliest ones, when he had stopped etching, and moving through to the present. Tamara and I are silent. The works grow progressively worse, becoming slapdash, ill-conceived. Arcady could be a good painter, but I don't think he cares any more. He's just keeping himself occupied, going through the motions of being an artist.

What has happened to him? Extreme poverty. It has inexorably taken over his life, drained his situation of hope. Although Arcady has exhibited widely and his works are held in many public collections, three factors unite to make it impossible for him to sell his work. Firstly, he is a regional artist, so the St Petersburg dealers, what there are of them, won't touch him. They have enough trouble looking after their own. Secondly, Russia has no moneyed middle class with surplus income to spend on artworks, so within Russia there is no market for art. The system of public art commissioning that characterised the Soviet era has now dwindled into insignificance. The only way to sell Russian art is to sell it abroad or to tourists within Russia. Which brings us to Arcady's third insurmountable obstacle. The Russian government has instituted a new law regarding the sale of art. This one attains new heights of skullduggery because it masquerades as governmental protectiveness. The new line is: 'We must keep our precious art in the country'. All Russian art is forbidden to leave Russia, except for the purposes of international museum exhibitions. This crazy law, which is of no benefit whatsoever to individuals or the country as a whole, is a psychological hangover from the paranoid mentality of the Iron Curtain days.

'Ever since Stalin, Russian government has continued to hate artists and intellectuals,' Tamara tells me. 'Always they invent new ways to control the artists. They must remain the underdogs.'

'But why?' I ask. 'What's the point now?'

'Because they are afraid of them. They think that in Russia artists and writers have big influence on people.'

There is only one way around this new law. If you purchase art from a reputable dealer, he will give you a certificate which you must then take to some bureaucratic department to have stamped. When you leave the country, you must present this certificate and the customs official may or may not let the work through. You just have to take the risk. But Arcady doesn't have a dealer. Again, this law is tantamount to preventing artists as individuals from selling

their work. Like thousands of other Russian artists, Arcady is trapped in hopeless poverty.

This sets the seal on my interest in purchasing one of Arcady's etchings. I'm now determined to do so. And I also understand and appreciate Pavel's conceptual paintings. I see that they are works of rage.

Arcady is very worried that I may have wasted the US$100 I've paid for one of his splendid etchings. Like all chronically depressed people, he worries too much. He's certain the work will be seized. Tamara tells me this money will keep him for two months. Arcady does receive a weekly disability pension from the Russian government. It's enough to buy food for one day. He teaches one day a week at the local art school, receiving, like the museum curators, a rate of pay less than menial workers.

———•◦•———

Tamara and I get off the train at Chernyshevskaya metro and walk the three blocks to the apartment she now lives in. It's the one near the Tauride Gardens she mentioned a few weeks ago. She held out for two months but then, I suspect through sheer exhaustion, accepted the impossibly of 'them' finding her an apartment right in the centre, like her previous one.

This neighbourhood was once aristocratic. Galina Petrovna and her husband, the philosopher, live only a few blocks away.

We turn into Tamara's street, a battle zone of watery trenches and heaped asphalt. There are no signs of workmen having been here recently — more deferred public works. A gloomy pall seems to hang over the whole street; the houses here are darker and plainer than the crumbling baroque ones in surrounding streets. Tamara's building is grim, its 'Dostoevski' courtyard, as she describes it, unutterably dreary. We walk into a gloomy corridor and the building swallows us up.

There are advantages to this new apartment. It's larger and her adult son now has a room of his own; it has its own small kitchen and quite a large bathroom with a badly abraded but attractive claw-footed Victorian bath. Yet I can see why Tamara's not happy here. Working with visual art, she is very sensitive to the aesthetics of her environment. Her temperament seems to have adjusted to the gloom of this place. The light of her old fire is slowly being extinguished. Though she always makes an effort publicly to inject energy into her encounters with others, as she has just done in Petrozavodsk, privately she's usually tired. She strikes me as being spiritually exhausted.

As soon as we enter the dark hallway and remove our coats and shoes I, too, feel depressed. The main room of the apartment, Tamara's room, is an ugly L-shape. Dim light from the courtyard filters through its one grubby window. Her paintings and shelves of books lent such charm to her old apartment, but here the effect is less than pleasing. The battered grand piano she never plays has been moved here too; I wonder if it belonged to her dead husband.

I go into the bathroom. Although I can wash here without fear of contamination, the lines of washing strung above the bath strike me as squalid and I make short work of freshening up.

I emerge to find Tamara in the L-shaped room, rummaging in bursting cupboards. I sit on the bed and look at the dirty glass of the window, remembering how light streamed through the windows of her other apartment and how they looked across at the elegant architecture of fashionable shops. That apartment engaged with the street; that's why this one's so miserable — it's like being locked up in the city's back cupboard.

'What'll we eat for lunch?' Tamara asks. 'Potatoes?' I say yes, knowing this is all she has, adding that I'm going to the shop across the road to get some mineral water. If I tell her I'm buying food, she'll forbid me — she considers it's her place to feed me — but after two days of carbohydrates I'm desperate for protein. When I return with the water, a wedge of cheese, tinned fish and a loaf of dark rye, she triumphantly brandishes what she's been looking for: a wad of Russian Museum posters.

'Ah!' she says, now scanning the cluttered shelves above her bed. 'I have something for you.'

She locates a box wrapped in brown paper and presents it to me. Inside is a set of delicately beautiful scalloped teacups and saucers scattered with hand-painted violets, made at St Petersburg's famous porcelain factory. Tamara has a single, chipped version of one of these cups and I'd commented on how lovely it was. That she has remembered this, and that she's bought me an entire set which she can ill afford, moves me almost to tears. She looks at me. 'I knew you loved these cups,' she says.

After lunch the purpose of the Russian Museum posters is revealed. Moving aside teetering stacks of books and papers, Tamara lays the posters out in a flat pile on the closed lid of the grand piano. She then takes the etching I bought from Arcady and carefully inserts it between the flattened posters, rolls the thin pile into a cylinder and then wraps it in crumpled brown paper.

'If they stop you at customs, you tell them it is just posters,' she says. She wraps the posters with a kind of glee; the old determined glint in her eye returns. I'm reminded of how, during Soviet times, the staff of the Russian Museum offered what protection they could to artists like Malevich and Filanov accused of 'formalist error'. They secretly, dangerously, stored their paintings in the bowels of the museum, preserving them for posterity. Decades later, Tamara is driven by this same instinct to protect Russian artists from officialdom. Judging by the efficiency with which she's hidden the etching, such procedures might be a normal part of her day.

SIBERIAN WOLF

———◆◆◆———

How can I injure this man sitting next to me, maim him for life? I watch words spill out of his smiling wet mouth; he's such an unctuous moron he thinks I'm charmed by him.

I look up and down the laden dinner table for inspiration, wishing I could just ram a fork in his eye. Anatole waves from one end, screws up his eyes wickedly and points his video camera at me. Tonight he and Irina are celebrating their twentieth wedding anniversary. Their vibrant living room, walls lined with charming portraits they've silk-screened of family and friends, is festive with decorations. They've invited about fifteen people over, including this loathsome toad and his thickset wife with bleached coke-queen hair who wears a ton of gold and diamonds — god, is all that real? — and scowls at me from across the table.

Boris, that's his name, greeted me in quite good English, so initially I was pleased when Irina considerately placed him next to me. Ada could enjoy herself without the burden of translating for me.

Boris is around thirty-five, dark with a ruddy complexion that's even redder tonight because he's flushed. I could tell straightaway he was elated about something.

He told me he and coke-queen had just returned from London. 'Very profitable business trip,' he said, glowing. His English is textbook precise. He claims to have spent part of his childhood in London but I don't believe him; his accent is American. I notice everything about him shines — hair, skin, white teeth — except his eyes. He has dead eyes.

'What kind of business are you in?' I asked.

'I am a fur trader,' he said.

I mentally recoiled, hating him already. Animals are one of the passions of my life, the chief one perhaps. I collect press cuttings about them, am moved to tears by stories of them, like the one about the lioness at an African game park who adopted and protected an orphaned baby oryx, a kind of antelope. How little we know about what animals feel, what they are capable of. I despise mankind for its Neanderthal hunting instincts. And now fate had placed Cro-Magnon man himself right next to me at a dinner table, Anatole and Irina's dinner table. What the hell was he doing here?

Behave, I told myself, staring at the potato salad on my fork and reasoning that fur trading had been a traditional occupation in Russia for centuries. Besides, here was a rare opportunity to get to know the Devil. 'Really?' I said. 'I've never met a fur trader before. What do you do exactly?'

'I buy skins directly from hunters or, how do you say, runners — you know, carriers, some people have this job — and sell them to international dealers, top dealers. The runners come to me from all over Russia, even across the borders. They bring me skins sometimes from far away. China. Asia.'

'You must be a very well-known fur trader,' I said, watching him preen like the self-important dolt he was.

'Very well known,' he agreed, slowly caressing the curve of his black eyebrow. 'I get good prices, so I pay well.'

'What kinds of animal skins do you deal in?' I asked.

'Bear, fox, Arctic fox, Siberian wolf, sometimes sable which is very good. The rarer the animal, the higher the price.'

Sable? Surely slaughter of sables wasn't still going on. 'Isn't it illegal to deal in protected species?' I asked.

'Sure,' he said sharply with a rolled American r.

'Sables are protected, aren't they?'

He waved away such concerns. 'Laws come and laws go,' he said breezily. 'Like fashion, you know what I mean? Five years ago women were nervous, very nervous, about wearing furs. Unless they lived in cold countries. But now all the models are wearing them and they're everywhere on, how do you say, catwalks. So everyone is wearing fur again. Men too.' He knocked back his vodka and poured himself another, not even noticing that my wine glass was empty. 'A month ago we got the most fantastic skin, very beautiful and very rare. This skin I just sold in London. This was just incredible. Fantastic.'

'What animal?' I asked, feeling sick.

'A panther, how do you say, leopard, from the Himalayas region.'

'A snow leopard?'

'Yes, that's right.'

'Snow leopards are nearly extinct.'

'Yes, yes,' he agreed enthusiastically. 'It has, how do you say, highest market value.'

'There's a market demand for the skins of snow leopards?' I asked, shocked. In Tibet this softest of leopards is worshipped as one of the reincarnations of the Buddha. Feeling nauseous, I put down my fork and pushed away the plate of food.

'Naturally.'

'But there's only a thousand of them left.'

'Now there are nine hundred ninety-nine,' he laughed.

It was at this point that I began to have thoughts of injuring him.

Now I refill my glass and sit there sipping.

'What were you paid for its fur?' I ask. I have to know.

He hesitates. He's not sure where this could lead. 'A very large sum,' he says.

'Ten thousand American dollars?' I say, mock wide-eyed, encouraging him to boast, thinking it will be an astronomical sum.

'Not bad. You're good,' he says, screwing up his eyes and nodding his head. He's beginning to sweat. 'English pounds.

Four thousand pounds,' he says proudly.

'Four thousand pounds!' I gasp. He thinks I'm impressed but I'm devastated. That this magical creature should have a price on its head at all is obscene, but for it to be such a paltry sum when it's on the brink of extinction! It's terrifying. 'I bet your wife's beautiful jewellery is worth nearly that much,' I say provocatively.

He gives a disdainful little laugh and looks across at the gleaming rocks above the purple nail polish. 'Cela's jewellery is worth much more than that,' he says arrogantly.

I glance across at her. Death has come to one of the world's rarest and most exquisite creatures so that this nasty cow can draw public attention to her fat neck by encircling it with diamond-sprinkled bands of gold.

I think of another Russian, a dangerous one, with a very different association with endangered animals. After three glasses of wine I become idealistic and wonder whether this man's story might act as some kind of example for Boris, set him thinking one day, plant a seed. Anything.

'Do you know any mafia guys in Moscow?' I ask him.

'Sure,' he says easily.

'There's one I really want to meet, but nobody here knows how to get in touch with him. He's famous in Moscow because his pal rides around in the back of his limo with him. Guess who his pal is.'

'Who?'

'A Siberian tiger.'

'No,' he laughs. 'You are joking with me.'

'No I'm not. I have a video of this man riding around with his tiger sitting up next to him. It sleeps with him every night. I brought the video with me. So you've never heard of this man?'

'No. He must be a crazy man.'

'Not at all. He's very, very intelligent, very strong. People are very afraid of him. But he's not afraid of anything. Nothing. And the tiger knows this.'

'Where does he get this tiger?'

'Why? Are you going to have it murdered for its fur?'

Isn't social interaction amazing? How can I joke with this worm? It must be the wine.

'No way,' he laughs.

'I'll tell you where he got it.' I pause. 'You know the Siberian tiger is nearly extinct?'

'Sure.'

'There are only five hundred of them in the wild?'

'Sure.'

'And the Russian government is doing nothing about this because there's no money or it doesn't care or whatever?'

'Sure.'

'There's a man who lives outside Moscow who does care. He's got this big compound and he's trying to breed the tigers in captivity so they won't die out. But this man has no money and things are very difficult for him. It gets to the point where he can't afford to feed the tigers …'

'He could have sold two for their skins to feed the rest.'

'No, Boris. If he's trying to build their numbers up because they're nearly extinct, he can't afford to kill two because with that kind of attitude pretty soon there'll be none left. No more Siberian tigers. No more snow leopards. And then how are people like you going to make a living? Have you ever thought about that?'

'Sure.'

I continue. 'The mafia guy gets to hear of the tiger project. He's curious and one day he drives out there. The project looks promising because one of the females has given birth to a tiger cub. But it doesn't look too healthy. He sums up the situation: the desperate keeper, the starving tigers, and he makes the keeper an offer he can't refuse. He'll pay for the entire captive breeding project, the tigers' food and upkeep and everything else, if he can have the sickly little cub.

'Since then everything's gone according to plan. The mafia guy reared the little cub himself and it's survived into adulthood. But he worries to death about it and continues to take it to every vet in Moscow. There's something wrong with its stomach, which nobody can seem to cure. But it's happy nevertheless. The tiger and the mafia guy go everywhere together. They're very attached to each other. What do you think of this?'

He shrugs. 'Crazy guy. But I can imagine how he uses that tiger to scare people.'

'No, he doesn't. That's not the point. The point is that the mafia guy really loves the tiger. He'll do anything for it. And the tiger knows this and he loves the mafia guy back. Can you understand that?'

He thinks. 'Some people like to have pets. If a tough guy has a pet, he wants it to be a scary animal.'

'And they say tigers are the scariest animal of all,' I say, 'that humans can't ever tame them, that you can never turn your back on them. But that's not true, is it? The mafia guy's proven you can be good friends with a tiger. You know, I really love the contrast between you and this guy, Boris. It's so Russian, the complete extremes and contradictions of character within each of you.'

'Yes?'

'The bad guy is trying to save a species from extinction, and you, the respectable businessman, you're out there killing them off.'

Boris laughs. He genuinely thinks it's a joke.

———————•—•—•———————

Curious as to why Anatole and Irina are friendly with Boris, I recount all this to Ada. She explains that Cela is a relative of one of them, I've forgotten which. But the story of the snow leopard upsets her and I wish I'd never mentioned it. Ada has enough on her mind at the moment

Living together during the weeks I've been here has brought Ada and Mitri closer together. Mitri has graduated from adoring admirer to trusted companion; even their bickering has a spirit of humour and easy intimacy. Mitri laughs at being told he's lazy and Ada shrugs and knows he'll never change.

Financially, however, their lives have fallen into a depressing slump. In the months before my arrival Mitri's business was doing well and he was earning up to US$2000 a month. But Russia has been borrowing too heavily from the United States, and the economy is now seriously in default. The value of the ruble has plummeted and Mitri's monthly income has dwindled to less than US$200. This requires him to buy more motor oil and spend more time in Moscow.

Ada must now be so careful with money, it's a daily preoccupation. She's losing something of her glow, doubtless through worry. She has come to stay with me because Mitri is away, and although she's as protective of me as ever, I occasionally detect a mild censoriousness in her manner toward me. Certainly she disapproves of my interest in Russia's animals.

Animals are everywhere in St Petersburg. Besides meeting the adored pets of people I visit, I encounter them daily in the streets and busy public areas. In the metro a marmalade cat rides the crowded trains and escalators, nestled unconcernedly against the chest of a boy of twelve or so. Through the window of an antiques shop in the Smolny district I occasionally catch sight of a noble grey dog — so like a wolf I'd swear he is one — lounging on baroque couches. Each day on Nevsky Prospekt an amiable, hoop-jumping German shepherd and his dainty companion, a pirouetting Pomeranian, perform their routines within snapping distance of the Persian kittens who wait patiently for buyers in the arms of matronly vendors.

Further afield, animals animate the deserted parks and surrounding woods of great palaces. As in any fairytale, these dark silent woods are inhabited by creatures friendly and frightening: russet squirrels that scurry across your path and dart up trees and wild black boars that lurk unseen.

I have only a short time left in St Petersburg so I've set aside today to explore the other animals of the city, the ones in the institutions devoted to them. As soon as I tell Ada this, her mood changes. I've brought coffee and my Italian coffee pot with me from Australia and have indoctrinated her into the joys of morning Lavazza, but this morning as we sit and sip at the small kitchen table she holds her head higher than usual and is silent. It's clear she doesn't wish me to go to the Leningrad Zoopark. She's vague about whether she's ever been there herself.

'Maybe. A long time ago,' she mutters tight-lipped, staring fixedly at some point above my head.

'Why don't you come with me?' I say, dismayed at this sudden rift but irritated at what I perceive as controlling behaviour.

'You know I must work.'

'But it's Saturday.'

'I must to prepare catalogue of exhibition devoted to two hundred years since killing Paul First,' she sniffs.

Like many animal lovers Ada avoids situations where she might have to confront suffering animals, wishing only to banish such thoughts from her mind. I understand how she feels, but I'm still determined to go to the zoopark.

The thought of St Petersburg's Museum of Zoology repels me even more. Museums that display animals as if they're rocks or minerals — insentient — rarely exist in the west these days. We've become ashamed of them.

This one, a colossal palace of enlightenment on Vasilevsky Island containing a comprehensive collection of every permutation of every fabulous creature ever known to man, so it seems, has changed little since the nineteenth century and is the finest in the world of the ones that remain.

Inside, there's a faded funfair feel about the place, a

nineteenth century Disneyland of creation's marvels.

Picture an armada of Noah's arks, and this will give you a sense of the sheer diversity and spectacle of exhibits in this museum. It's staggering. I walk through room after room of showcases, hundreds of them, crowded with stuffed animals and birds, each devoted to a species: an encyclopaedic display of exotically beautiful furs and feathers, so dangerous to their owners because so coveted by humans — the jungle cat patterns of ocelots, civets, servals, jaguars; the gorgeous plumage of macaws, toucans, rosellas; the luxuriant softness of Arctic fox, silver fox, sable.

Upstairs, amidst a paradise of pinned butterflies, I discover the smoky Lycaenidae, Nabokov's specialty, whose underwings he compared to Lolita's eyes.

Some of the animals are so wonderfully strange I don't recognise them. They may now be extinct, like the Tasmanian tiger in one of the Australian showcases. Its stuffed carcass is rotting, one wizened paw absurdly propped up by a rock. The condition of the other thousands of stuffed animals is excellent, even though many would be more than a century old, some two centuries as they once formed part of Peter the Great's *wunderkammer*.

The museum's pièce de résistance is a mammoth, dug up a few decades ago after being preserved for millennia in the Siberian ice. With his great upturned yellow tusks and rotting proboscis, he sits back on his haunches on a heap of fake ice in an enormous refrigerated showcase.

Mammoths fascinated me as a child because they had become extinct. The reason for this, it seemed to me, was because they'd lived so long ago. Extinction spoke of eons, periods of time so vast that the concept of time itself was rendered incomprehensible. Little did I then know that in my lifetime, less than a millisecond in the cosmic calendar, many of the animals that defined the world and roamed my imagination — lions, tigers, gorillas, giraffes, bears — would be on the brink of extinction. I would have found this idea as incomprehensible as the eons of time it took for the mammoth to become extinct.

One aspect of this museum is distinctly weird — its comprehensive displays of domestic animals. I'm shocked at this, as if our emotional attachment to pets somehow makes them taboo in a museum of animals. Entire vitrines are devoted to permutations of everything from English hunting dogs to long-haired domestic cats. Some displays make a scientific point, like one that traces the evolution of the dog from the wolf to the German shepherd, but the majority are mere catalogues of the infinite variety of colour and patterning: stripes on tabby cats or spots on Bengals. This stamp-collecting mentality extends throughout the museum. A magnificent white peacock, perched so that all of its splendid tail is visible, dominates a large vitrine devoted entirely to pure white birds.

Bears come in for a major essay in colour coding: grizzly bears, honey bears, brown bears and an appealing long-haired one like a hybrid panda-honey bear. All of these bears, among them three tiny cubs, were killed so the museum visitor could be made aware of the variety of the colours of their coats.

Entire families of animals have been killed to achieve these impressive displays; entire packs of wolves, prides of lions, colonies of penguins. One cub in a family of Siberian tigers is amazingly tiny, not much bigger than a domestic kitten; it can only have been a few hours old when its life was extinguished.

When these groups of animals were hunted down over a century ago, the natural world was regarded as vast and indestructible, its supply of exotic creatures endlessly bountiful. Enormous dioramas with their props and painted backdrops simulate the habitats of animals in the wild. Later, at the zoo-park, I'm struck by the irony of such careful attention being paid to the natural environments and companionship of stuffed animals, while living ones despondently eke out their solitary days in tiny concrete cages. The diorama of the African savanna with its pride of lions is four times the size of the lion's cage at the zoo. The stuffed snow leopard at the zoology museum crouches on a rocky outcrop against a vast panorama of mystical mountains, while at the zoo the living one dozes on a high makeshift shelf just wide enough for it to lie on, the end of its splendid long tail trailing on the cement below. As so few of them now remain in existence, the one in St Petersburg should perhaps be grateful to be alive — if lying on a green-painted wooden bench all day can be called being alive.

Ironically, the museum, this mausoleum of tens of thousands of creatures slaughtered in the name of science, carries the message that animals are beautiful and creation sublime. The message of the Leningrad Zoopark, where the beauty of living animals is eclipsed by their distress, is quite the reverse.

Unlike the rest of St Petersburg, the Leningrad Zoopark has retained its Soviet name, which is appropriate given its brutal Soviet architecture and prominent padlocks.

On the way there, crossing the Trotsky Bridge to the Petrograd side of St Petersburg, I walk through the Peter and Paul Fortress, which is presided over by the eagle, emblem of tsarist Russia. In each room I encounter its majestic form, either fashioned from precious materials like marble and bronze, or resplendent with gilt and jewels; even royal costumes and textile hangings have eagles embroidered on them. Russia's eagle kills the Roman and American ones: it has two heads, doubly fierce, all the better to watch you with.

Inside the bleak entrance of the zoopark the first creature I encounter is an eagle. This is a living one, a poor bedraggled bird tethered by a short grimy rope to a railing, a trace of majesty only in its size. A young woman comes over and unties one end of the rope, a signal for visitors to converge on the spot. The eagle sits disconsolately on her wrist, eyeing the humans it is to entertain. When I leave the zoo several hours later, it's still being passed from arm to outstretched arm, obediently suffering its speckled feathers to be stroked by hand after hand.

The old lion is outraged at his decades of imprisonment in a tiny concrete cage. He sits behind its bars and roars out his anguish. A couple of kids respond to his roars with shrieks of laughter while their parents smile indulgently. He eyes them disdainfully, rises arthritically onto his haunches and shifts his gaze to the large padlock dangling in front of his nose. This provokes high-pitched squeals of delight. Such a magnificent beast, reduced to an eczema-splotched laughing-stock.

The Bengal tiger has gone mad. Splashes of sunlight move across her richly striped coat as she relentlessly paces her small L-shaped prison with its wire-mesh-reinforced bars. Eight paces along one side of the cage, turn the corner, six paces along the other side till she hits the wall with its stupid mock jungle of childishly painted trees, turn, six paces back to the corner, turn, eight paces to the wall, turn. She does this all day. The manic pacing rhythm is interrupted briefly when she slips in her own urine and she too provokes explosions of laughter. The dappled sunlight, the bars, the mesh, the moving yellow and brown tiger stripes and the dumb painted trees blur impressionistically into a crazy kinesis. Watching her, I inter-pret her pacing as signalling distress and frustration. It's not till I return to Australia and read *A Different Nature*, David Hancock's wonderful book about animals and zoos, that I understand years of close confinement, concrete and boredom have driven this highly intelligent animal insane.

An exhibition of children's paintings of the zoo's animals, on display in a long, low shed in the grounds, gives me an inkling of why those kids found the distressed lion so amusing. The paintings are joyous, as if the children are painting not the miserable occupants of the zoo, but their idea of animals as wondrous, endearingly different, beautifully strange, excitingly fierce. They seem to be expressing an innate love of animals, some forgotten sense of kinship. Two cheerful giraffes converse on the shores of a lake, while outside the real giraffe is dejectedly alone in her bare enclosure. A painted tiger with a green-eyed watchful gaze lurks behind foliage, predatory and still as night, unlike the poor mad thing outside. A lion's head resembles a sun, its golden mane bursting around it like rays.

Walking around this dismal zoo, I'm initially tempted to think of it as a metaphor for the Soviet treatment of human beings, but the plight of the animals themselves takes precedence. The analogy stands nevertheless. Judged by the standards to which zoos in the west have evolved, this is a concentration camp. Each animal has its personal response to day after day of cement and excruciating boredom. A mandrill clings desperately to a wire door high up in his cage, giving it a thorough shaking every few minutes. He's loosened the tin Pepsi sign above his head, one of several on various cages, including the lion's. In a direct appeal, a monkey stretches his amazingly human-like arm through the bars of his cage and sits with it dangling outside, his eyes averted from the padlock that is larger than his face. Nearby a pair of meerkats sits up watching anxiously: they're used to semidesert and here they can't burrow in the hard cement, so they're in a permanent state of anxiety. At least they have each other, unlike the majority of the zoo's solitary animals.

Tamara lent me a book recently by a Russo-American journalist. Entitled *Escape from Ward Six*, it chronicles Stalin's crimes against the Russian people. One chapter explores how Russia's monasteries were desecrated and turned into psychiatric hospitals. Used as dumping grounds for dissidents, these so-called hospitals became notorious for their inhuman abuse of patients. When I first turned the book's pages and came across a series of photographs of emaciated patients, I instinctively averted my eyes. Forcing myself to look, I saw that some patients were caged, naked and obviously lobotomised. That human beings could be reduced to this. Some of the animals in this zoo remind me of those harrowing photographs, the ones who, spiritually exhausted like concentration camp victims, have given up. They sit or lie listlessly all day, closed in upon themselves in some gloomy netherworld. Of all these unutterably sad creatures, the golden jackal is perhaps the most poignant. A pack animal, a solitary existence holds no meaning for him. He sits as if willing himself into nonexistence, his skin shrinking back into his bones.

The grim cement enclosures of the Leningrad Zoopark reflect what Stalin's hidden agenda seems to have been: to reduce existence itself to a punishable offence. The totalitarian structures of the mountain goat enclosure, Soviet mountain passes, bring tears to my eyes, tears of pity for the goats scaling towering concrete loops and tears of laughter at the absurdity of it. It's very late in the afternoon. I'm clearly hysterical.

As I leave, a woman comes up to the patient old dromedary waiting near the entrance to give rides to children. She gives it a bread roll and kisses it, leaving a bright lipstick mark on its face.

———•◦•———

The zoo and its 'cash problems' make the front page of the *St Petersburg Times*. I pick up a copy on my way to visit the apartment-museum of Sergei Kirov, St Petersburg's popular governor whom Stalin had murdered in 1934, which I find is luxuriously carpeted with polar bears. On the way there I also

270

discover that my photographs of the Museum of Zoology and the zoopark are ready, so I don't stay long.

I sort through the photographs, laying them out in groups all over the bed, the sofa, the floor, and become absorbed in this task. Felix sits and watches with interest, his little arched head following the movement of my hands, occasionally jumping on a photograph and sending it skidding. The hours pass.

Mahatma Gandhi said a nation can be judged by the way it treats its animals. I wonder what the zoopark says about St Petersburg. The question is answered in part by the *Times* article. The director is quoted as saying that his priority is to save its 410 species and 3000 animals from 'extinction' — an interesting choice of word. The rest is a familiar tale. Officially the zoo and its animals are revered. I read that during the 900 day Siege of Leningrad, 'a time when people were eating stray cats, rats and dead relatives, the animals in the zoo were never considered dinner'. But the zoo has been beleaguered since the 1960s when plans to restore it 'ran aground financially'. Continuing sponsorship from Pepsi seems unlikely. The director's one hope is that 'money will roll in from abroad'. Eleven magnificent eagle owls, an East Siberian subspecies, are among the animals the zoopark is offering for adoption or sale.

I hear a key turn in the lock of the second steel door and look around at the sea of photographs of stuffed and despairing animals. Caught red-handed. As the key turns in the lock of the third steel door I have a sudden instinct to sit on the worst group of images or distract Ada from coming into the room, but this is, of course, ridiculous. I sit there like a hypnotised chicken, expecting the axe of outrage to fall at any minute.

To my relief Ada goes straight into the kitchen. I call her name and follow her in there.

'Ach, I thought you would still be at Kirov Museum.'

'I went there this morning. Let's have some tea.' I fill a pockmarked saucepan with water. It's getting dark outside and the kitchen's gloomy, but this is preferable to the harsh neon of the electric light.

Ada goes into the hall to hang up her coat, then returns, sitting at the table, chin on hand.

'What do you do this afternoon?' she asks me.

'I went to that European supermarket at Passazh and bought some chicken for dinner and some cream cheese. It's quite a good supermarket.'

'It is for Americans. Very expensive. I tell you not to go there.'

I open the fridge. 'Let's have some of the cheese now.'

'What else do you do?'

'Oh I don't know, Ada. Just waffled around, reading the paper and things.'

Ada watches me spread creamy white cheese onto biscuits. I check that the knob's turned on high: water takes forever to boil on the ancient stove. 'What did *you* do today?'

'Continue my work on catalogue of many engravings for Paul First exhibition and now I must to make the cucumbers.' She rises, puts on an apron, washes some long oily strands of a dill-like herb, puts them on the small kitchen table and begins chopping. Ada never relaxes.

'You are very naughty not to show me anything you write,' she says as she sprinkles salt on a pile of cucumbers.

Never underestimate the intuition of a Russian woman.

'I told you. It's only a journal. You'll have to wait until I work out what I'm going to do with it.'

'I think you do not tell me the truth. I think you are writing bad things about Russia.'

This from Ada, who has told me so many bad things about Russia.

'You know, I would not like to think that someone would write such things.'

'Oh all right then, Ada, I'll find something to show you.' I sigh irritably, stride into the living room and sit on the bed, peeved, offended, western concepts of artistic freedom ringing in my ears, my face getting hot. I'll write what I please. Coincidentally, I've just been reading about Pushkin's torments at the hands of the tsar's censors in the 1830s. Censorship comes as naturally to Russians as salting cucumbers. Is this the same Ada who wakes me with, 'Good morning, my darling?' I picture this Ada and guilt enters my mix of emotions.

I take a deep breath and consider, a little appalled at myself for being so angry with her. Perhaps it's more than the Russian instinct for censoring others that's driving Ada, perhaps it's an atavistic instinct as well, the unspoken bargain where a guest honours his host by not speaking ill of him or his country. Ada's entitled to this kind of respect from me.

In any case, it's ludicrous to hide the truth from her. I return to the kitchen with the *St Petersburg Times*.

'You've only started worrying about me writing bad things since I went to the zoo. Is that what's worrying you?'

'You go to zoo twice,' she sulks, referring to my returning there to take photographs.

'Well the zoo's in trouble. Read this.' I thrust the article under her nose. She sits down and reads it very carefully, frowning, shaking her head and making *tch* noises.

She looks up at me and sighs wearily. 'This is so terrible. Is this what you write about?'

'I don't know. I'm looking at photographs at the moment, thinking.'

'What photographs? Show me.' Ada's always excited at the prospect of photographs, precious items that are so expensive to have developed.

'Some of them are upsetting, Ada, I'm warning you.'

'Why do you do this?' she asks mournfully.

'You must try not to take it so personally. I don't want to attack Russia or St Petersburg. The zoo here and the zoological museum, they're tied up with the whole history of human attitudes to animals, humans everywhere.'

'Show me photographs.'

She heads for the living room. I follow her, a sinking feeling in my stomach.

'So many,' she breathes, scanning the room wide-eyed. She picks up photograph after photograph, lingering over the ones at the zoo — so many animals with their noses pressed against the wire of their cages — crying out 'Oh, so terrible' when she comes across the bony, listless jackal, who in the photograph resembles an emaciated corpse, hardly a jackal at all. 'What is this animal?'

'A golden jackal.'

'Where it comes from?'

'Africa. The desert.'

'St Petersburg is very cold place for this African animal.'

'Yes. Look how beautiful the coat of this lynx is,' I say, handing her a stuffed museum specimen, terrified she's going to burst into tears. She nods and scans the photographs, picking up one of a Siberian wolf.

'This is Siberian wolf, very beautiful. You know, when I was a small child in Tomsk and took trips into Siberian countryside, I saw a few times this wolf with his family in the forest. I was very frightened but he does not come near us. He just watches. He is very clever this wolf.'

'And do you ever see them now?' I ask.

'No, not now. They disappear. This Siberian wolf is very healthy,' she says, pleased.

'This is a stuffed wolf, Ada.'

'No. He is alive.'

'Look at the fake snow. You can see part of the showcase.'

We look at the handsome, intelligent face of the wolf. He

looks like the leader, an island of calm, seated with his paws outstretched amidst the snarling, biting, glowering-eyed members of his pack.

'I don't believe it. He look more alive than living … golden jackal.'

'You see. St Petersburg's Museum of Zoology had the best taxidermists.' I point to a group of photographs of snarling bears, cheetahs and gorillas, their terrifying pounces and roars fixed forever inside their display cases. 'They look so real, but they're taxidermists' artworks. Look at the bears.' Big grizzlies loom and snarl menacingly while cubs roll playfully in the undergrowth. 'They've stuffed them so their expressions resemble all the moods humans associate with them. They would have been limp corpses when the taxidermists received them and they've transformed them into predatory beasts threatening to humans, so that's how we think of wild animals and remember them.'

'So is okay to kill animal because he kill you?'

'Exactly. Even the poor old Tasmanian tiger is snarling like some killer, but in Australian we were the killers who hunted him into extinction.'

'This one is … no more?'

'No. Nevermore.'

'*Tch.*' She shakes her head sorrowfully. 'So what are you thinking about all this?' she asks.

I shrug. How to put the feeling into words. 'It's like when you and Tamara take me to your palaces. So often I experience

St Petersburg as a city haunted by the ghosts of a beautiful, lost world. And in the present, for living people, day-to-day existence is such a struggle. This is true of the animals as well, but in a more universal way. The zoology museum is like a palace of a lost world too, one that existed not so long ago, a time of magical forests and mysterious jungles teeming with hundreds of different kinds of wonderful animals, and we thought this world would always be like that and never change, that it was indestructible, which is probably how the St Petersburg elite was regarded. And the occupants of the museum, they're long dead but exquisite, just like your poets and princesses. Then you go to the zoo and see that existence for the living animals is such a struggle, and the poor things look so mangy and exhausted. They have a Soviet past hanging over them, just like you. But it goes beyond that. The zoopark and the condition of the animals there is like a symbol of the sorry state of the wild animals of the world.' I sigh. 'Do you understand what I mean?'

She tilts her head back and eyes me. 'So, if you write about terrible state of animals you will say it is whole world and not only Russia.'

'Yes.'

UDACHI

—◆—

Irina and Anatole, as arranged, appear at the apartment, greeting me with a volley of Russian, kisses and expressive gestures. Irina carries a large apple-green umbrella and a bouquet of orange and red flowers. Anatole carries the video camera and a loudly diamond-patterned garment. I put the garment on, as indicated by Irina, and discover it's the top half of a harlequin outfit. I grab a glass, pour red wine into it and follow them in the pale sunlight across cracked paths and muddy weeds to the few stunted, scrappy trees outside the entrance to their apartment building. Here I sit in an orange plastic chair they've placed under a tree for me. I place the glass at my feet. Irina opens the green umbrella and hands it to me, together with the bunch of flowers. Anatole slips the mike in my collar, lines up the shot and he and Irina confer. Irina indicates for me to hold the flowers higher and the umbrella back further. She arranges my hair on my shoulders and looks to Anatole. He nods his satisfaction. Action.

'Hello Ada my darling, I must ask you to translate for me one last time when Anatole plays this for all of you after I've gone home. Mitri, you cuddly Russian bear, I hear your dreams are about to come true and that you and Ada are planning to get married. I wish you both every happiness. Give my love to Novimira and Vassily and thank your father for the lovely Dostoevski book. The Soviet magazines on collective farming are pretty amazing too. Tell Vassily I understand the contrast.

'If I was granted one wish, it would be to take you all back to Melbourne with me and live with you as neighbours in the one street. But even though you would have high salaries and colour reality TV, I know you wouldn't be happy there. You all love St Petersburg too much. For these past months you've all welcomed me into your lives as a friend and I have never before experienced such a community of wonderfully generous and intelligent people.

'I came here because I'm in love with Russian art and writing and the romantic extremes of its history. But there's always been something else, some intangible attraction. Now I know what it is. It's Russian people. It's all of you, your warmth and strength and love of beauty. Before, I'd only glimpsed Russian people in your literature. Now, thanks to you, I've experienced what it's like to live among Russians. It's been exhilarating — so fascinating, moving, amusing, crazy and scary.' I hesitate. Anatole peers around the camera at me with raised eyebrows and flicks his moustache. What's the hold-up? 'I'm talking about you, Anatole, you sexy man, you divinely grumpy, troublemaking Vertov. You're the soul of Russian anarchy and St Petersburg intelligence. The intoxicating complexity of it all makes my Arfstraalian head spin. Thank you for your eye-opening gift of that book.

'If I'd been here alone, I'd have spent most of my time looking at beautiful and strange things and photographing them. This would have been pleasant but superficial. You've all taught me to see Russia's rich culture partly through your eyes, so it's been brought to life for me. Irina, your love for your family and friends shines through in your brilliant textile portraits of them. I have only to look at them to understand that in Russia art is not separate from life, as it is in the west. I'd love to be able to speak with you and please forgive me for not learning Russian. Tamara, for me Dostoevski is now forever associated with your beautiful face on that white night. I'll always think of you as the soul of St Petersburg. I loved your old apartment, but mostly because it was you, so maybe the new one doesn't matter so much. Thank you for Kizhi and everything else, especially Ekaterina and Ivanov. Please thank Ekaterina for the lovely shawl she crocheted for me. Tell her this kind of traditional garement has become very fashionable in the west.

'Ada, you've watched over my days like a guardian angel and no traveller in a faraway land could wish for a better one. You've been my interpreter, guide, tour organiser, friend, sister, protector and occasionally mother — at times a disapproving one, but then I'm such a wayward child. I can never thank you enough, but, still, a thousand thanks for making one of the great experiences of my life possible.

'You remember I visited Galina Petrovna? Her husband is a philosopher — I think I told you this — and he said something I can't forget. He told me how the elite and intelligentsia of St Petersburg had been extinguished in the decades following the revolution, and he asked himself if, because of this, St Petersburg could still be said to exist. He said something like, "What is a city? Is a city its buildings or its people?" If he asked me this now, I'd suggest he accompany Tamara on a walk through Dostoevskian streets and then you, Ada, on a trip, to Gatchina perhaps, where you'd show him the tapestries and gilt furnishings recently placed in its vast rebuilt interiors. I'd suggest he visit a class where Anatole is teaching age-old silk-screening techniques, and then have his portrait woven by Irina as he listens to Mitri reciting poems by Lermontov. Then he'd understand that St Petersburg is still very much alive, that it has protectors like you.'

I place the flowers in my lap and, reaching down, pick up the wine and toast the camera. 'Here's to St Petersburg and here's to all of you. *Udachi*.'

'*Udachi*,' chorus Irina and Anatole, delighted I've spoken a word they can understand.

While Anatole puts away the props, Irina takes my hand and leads me into their living room. I sit on the couch, tickling their white cat. Irina pours two glasses of fruit juice and we clink glasses. She pushes a package toward me, indicating that I'm to open it. Inside is a traditional Russian ostrich-sized wooden egg which Irina has made herself, a joyous object with a hand-painted bird of good tidings and folk art style decoration. It's actually a container, the two halves fitting together. I begin to swivel it, looking questioningly at Irina. Yes, she nods, open it: like a Fabergé egg it contains a surprise. Nestled inside is a beautiful little book made of cloth, photographs and sketches of St Petersburg buildings on the covers. I flick through the pages and the circle of friends smile out at me, in group shots and individual portraits. Oh, if only I could tell Irina how apt this is, how her gift resounds with what I've just said to the video camera: that Russia's culture drew me here and the surprise discovery was all of them. Irina is bright-eyed with the pleasure of giving me these lovely things.

I'm still looking at them and thanking her, a little misty-eyed, when Anatole arrives bearing more gifts: a large, green apple, solid glass with a white glass leaf, which feels so sensuously round to hold, and an enormous pure silk scarf with a silk-screened pattern of medieval women wearing *kokoshniki*, those majestic headdresses that rise to a point. He, too, made both things.

At last it strikes me what superb craftspeople these two are. Unlike most makers in the west, they're not limited to one medium; they can work with wood or glass or textiles and they're virtuoso sketchers and painters as well. Not to mention video artists.

Hours later I'm standing with Ada, Mitri, Tamara and Anatole on the platform of St Petersburg's Moscow Station, where they've come to see me off. I'm feeling a little teary and shaky, only partly because of Anatole's maniacal driving. He and Mitri carry my luggage into my compartment and I file back out with them for final hugs, kisses and promises to return. I hate farewells and return to the train, standing in the corridor. We pull faces and blow kisses through the glass. Mitri puts his arm protectively around Ada and she leans into him, smiling into my eyes as if there's a secret between us. To my amazement, Tamara begins to cry; tears stream down her cheeks. This sets me off. Anatole grimaces in mock disgust at such displays of emotion and indicates that I should dab my face with the silk scarf I'm wearing, his gift. Thank god he didn't bring his video camera. The train pulls out. Waves and kisses. Goodbye goodbye.

I go into the compartment and sit near the window, looking out, feeling drained. An attendant brings around a plastic package of food and I sit there chewing, so preoccupied I don't notice what I'm eating. For the first time in three months I'm truly alone. I feel as if I've returned to myself. The train picks up speed and St Petersburg flashes by. I heave a great shuddering sigh and a kind of gloom settles on me. It's the rupture, the leave-taking from a community of people I've grown used to being among. I picture Ada on the station platform, her enigmatic smile.

A man taps me on the arm, speaking in Russian, and I see that he wants to pull down the bed above me. This is a sleeping compartment with four beds. Another man with tattoos all over his arms is beginning to get undressed. Oh great. I'm in a sleeping compartment with three strange men, none of whom speaks English. This feels distinctly uncomfortable. At least they're all strangers to each other.

But they're polite. By the usual means, smiles and sign language, we work out that I'll take a top bunk, which seems safer to me somehow. I climb up and surreptitiously remove some of my clothes so that I can sleep comfortably.

One of them slides the door closed. There's a complicated-looking catch on the door and he fiddles with it until the door locks. Christ, now I'm trapped in here with the three of them. I've no idea how to undo that lock. He clicks the light off. It's pitch black. I don't even know where the light switch is. I search the blackness for the suggestion of a shape. Nothing. Being in this bed, hemmed in by the dark, so close to the ceiling, is like being in a coffin. Another entrapment scenario.

I lie in the blackness waiting for the old sickly feeling that signals the onset of panic. It doesn't come. I actually feel quite serene and sleepy. I yawn.

I think of home. I've been away for over four years. Melbourne will always be home, but for the first time in my life I have no actual home to return to. No home, no job, and very little money. Only a lot of furniture, books and paintings and two fabulous cats, and nowhere to put any of it, them.

I don't seem to be bothered in the least by this, which surprises me.

My time in St Petersburg has dispelled my old fears. All of them. The neurotic terror of being trapped, and that insidious anxiety about what the future holds which I have for years busily placed on the back burner. That quietly gnawing species of anxiety, so familiar it's practically friendly.

Pffff. Evaporated.

I lie in the rattling blackness fathoming how this has occurred. I think of Ada and Tamara and the terrors and darknesses they've survived. To say I've been touched by them, brushed by the depths of their experience, and that my life in Melbourne will be easy compared to their lives in St Petersburg, is true but an oversimplification. There are myriad reasons, the entire St Petersburg experience. I breathe in this new sense of myself. My mind feels spacious. Luxuriating in the sudden freedom from plans involving other people, the sheer peace of it, I fall asleep anticipating the pleasure of journeying back to my St Petersburg friends in thought.

ACKNOWLEDGMENTS

———◆◆◆———

I owe the publication of this book to Erica Sanders, who acted as my agent, and Jo Paul, Commissioning Editor at Allen & Unwin, who believed in it. Their advice and encouragement throughout has been inspirational and my first thanks go to the both of them. I also thank Julia Stiles for her precise and sensitive editing, and for her helpful indications on refining the shape of the book.

There would be no *Letters from St Petersburg* without the people of that city who were my generous companions for several months. My deep affection and gratitude go to Olga Vlasova, Alexander Belashov, Liudmila Vostervsova, Anatole Rubzov and Irina Rubzov. I am also indebted to Natasha Vershinina, Marina Stekolnikova, Arcady Mozorov, Irina Sosnovczeva, Dimitry Ivanov and family, and the many other Russians who welcomed me into their homes or workplaces. A special thank you to my dear friend Yvonne Rees-Pagh, who made it all possible.

The support and friendship of Mary Ryllis Clark during the writing process made it that much more enjoyable. I thank her for reading each chapter on completion, for her useful comments and warm encouragement.

In matters of translation I am grateful to Dr Judith Armstrong for amending the Russian phrases in this book, and Galina Kordin-Dindas for transcribing Russian texts for me.

The freedom to write *Letters from St Petersburg* was provided by grants from the Literature Fund of the Australia Council, and Arts Victoria. My heartfelt thanks to both funding agencies, whose assistance also enabled me to return to St Petersburg for further research. A Varuna Fellowship from the Eleanor Dark Foundation provided a peaceful and supportive environment during the book's development phase. I particularly wish to thank Peter Bishop, Varuna's director, whose interest in Russian literature sparked some ideas.

One of the great pleasures of this project has been working with the staff at Allen & Unwin. I thank them all, in particular Catherine Taylor, Marie Baird, Catherine Milne, Zoe Sadokierski, Stephanie Whitelock, and Ellie Exarchos for her energetic design of the cover image.

Thanks are also due to Claire Gorman, a vital link in the chain of four.

My last and most personal thank you goes to my son Remen, whose love and strength of character have contributed vitally to this book.